With a Book in Her Hand

Robert L. Hiett

Published by Robert Hiett, 2023.

WITH A BOOK IN HER HAND

First edition. May 12, 2023.

ISBN: 979-8223658344

Written by Robert L. Hiett.

Preface

This was supposed to be a book about my mother, Mary Louise Ray Hiett. Now that I have read through the words I have written, I realize it's about a lot more. It's about the journey of faith of an ordinary (but deeply intellectual) woman from her young adult years in the southern U.S. until the end of her life in 2022. It's about the ideas that influenced her as evidenced by the books she cherished and kept until the end of her life. And, of course, it's a little bit about me.

As I have read over what I have written, it seems to me I have made her out to be a bit more saint-like than she really was. But if your own son won't treat you as saint-like, who will? And after one's death, perhaps it's all right to file the negative things away in the back of the cabinet. I see no purpose in recounting all the ways she could be difficult and demanding. I understand that many readers who knew her well will remember her differently than I have described. That's okay. I can only tell what I know of the story. Others can tell their own.

In this work I have referenced a wide array of the books Mom had collected over the course of her lifetime. I have decided not to try and footnote every reference to these works, but I have given the name of each work and author in the text. There is a selected bibliography at the end for those wishing to acquire some of these books on their own.

Readers should be aware that some of the source material regarding authors and their writings I have supplemented by using ChatGPT, an AI resource that acts as a more sophisticated search engine. The sources it cites for this book include the *Encyclopedia Britannica*, biographical websites, and the books I am referencing. There seems to be no standard way to footnote ChatGPT, so I have not included any.

I wish to thank those who encouraged and helped me in this endeavor. I include in that my wife of 60 years, Jane, along with my brother Jack and his wife Pat.

Introduction

In the early morning of Saturday, April 24, 2021, Mary Louise Ray Hiett, at the age of 97, boarded a medical transport bus outside her apartment on the west side of Fort Worth, Texas. It was the beginning of a 24-hour journey that would take her from her beloved Texas to Concord, North Carolina, where she would live out her days. It was bittersweet. Fiercely independent, she wasn't happy about leaving the city she had called home for more than 70 years. She would miss her church. She would miss her friends. She would miss the sights and sounds of the state in which she was born and the city in which she lived her entire adult life.

But she also knew that, at the age of 97, she needed a little help. She had mostly outlived her savings. She could no longer drive. Her laptop frequently acted up. Shopping was difficult. She couldn't always work the buttons on the TV remote controls. COVID hit, and her independent living facility imposed a lockdown. Only God knew how long that would last or even if she would survive it.

After much soul searching by all concerned, she agreed to move to North Carolina to live with me and my wife Jane. With the much-needed help of the internet and my brother Jack and his wife Pat, who lived in California, we found a transport company who could bring her from Texas to the East Coast. This firm offered medical care if it were needed and could negotiate COVID state boundary closures that were impeding travel across some state lines during the early months of the pandemic. The cost was high, but our options were limited.

Mary packed her apartment about as well as a 97-year-old can do. She carried with her a few bags containing clothes, medicine, and other sundries she would need right away in her new home. Jack and Pat volunteered to travel to Fort Worth once her living facility eased its COVID restrictions to pack up the remaining items. She arrived at her new home early Sunday morning, April 25.

The following June Jack and Pat drove to Fort Worth to close the apartment. Using their phone's Facetime app, they worked with Mom to identify the things that needed to be shipped to North Carolina and to determine which things could go to charity or be thrown away.

I was shocked when the first shipment arrived at our home. I was expecting a few more clothes and maybe some artwork, memorabilia, small appliances, and the like. Instead, she had arranged for them to ship eight boxes of books and an iron skillet.

+++++

Mom was born on April 20, 1923, in Abilene, Texas. Her father, Robert Latham Ray, worked in the tire business and moved the family to Dallas. Mary lived there with her mother, Louie Mae Lowry Ray, and two older brothers, Robert and Charles. The family was well to do, she told me before she died, living in a large Dallas home with a gardener/driver and housekeepers. This idyllic period ended, however, with the suicide of her father in December of 1929, in part a result of the failure of his tire business in the early years of the depression.

Louie, known to us all as "Granny", was left impoverished by these events and moved the family to Breckenridge, Texas, where Granny's parents were living. Granny's father operated a small grocery store. Unfortunately, the store went bankrupt because Granny's father would not refuse food to starving families unable pay in the depths of the Great Depression. Over the next few years of the Depression Granny eked out a meager existence for the family as a seamstress. Mary got a job working at a local ice cream parlor during her high school years. In the last months of her life, she spoke fondly of that experience, saying the owner of the store had taught her much about the value of hard work and self-reliance.

Mary graduated from Breckenridge High School in May 1940. By this time her older brother Robert had joined the U.S. Army Cavalry and Charles was working for a grocery store chain. Charles encouraged mother to attend college and, in a great act of kindness and generosity, paid her expenses for the first year.

Unfortunately, World War II intervened. Mary's high school sweetheart, Wallace Hiett, was sent to California where he was in training to work for Consolidated Aircraft as a sheet metal worker. She joined him in California, and they were married in Yuma, Arizona on November 1, 1941. Dad eventually joined the U.S. Marines and spent the war as an aircraft radio repairman in Southern California. He received his discharge from the Marines on May 5, 1946. They returned to Fort Worth where Dad entered the dry-cleaning business with his father and brother.

+++++

Mom was a life-long Christian, having made a faith commitment as a child in a Southern Baptist Church. In 1994, at the age of 71, she wrote a one-page account of her personal faith journey. I include it here because it seems more authentic than anything I could write:

Early Childhood: Cliff Temple Baptist Church (Dallas)

A Little Dutch girl dressed in blue, with a white cap and wearing a pair of wooden shoes (now wherever did those little wooden shoes come from?). And then there was BYPU (Baptist

*Young People's Union). The leadership didn't provide for a pianist and I could play "Bringing in the Sheaves," so we sang that one hymn every Sunday evening. Baptized by Dr. Wallace Bassett. Did I believe that Jesus is Lord? As surely as I believed the sun rises in the morning. The question was not the lordship of Christ, but rather the **decision** to become a member of the Church Family of God. I had this little Jewess friend named Beth Singer and I was allowed to visit synagogue school with her and I thought I might want to be a member of the Synagogue Family of God. I just hadn't noticed that their scriptures ended as ours continued!*

<u>Teen Years: First Baptist Church (Breckenridge, Texas)</u>

*Learning about the work of the Holy Spirit through the experiential "Yes". One sermon stands out: The Wages of Sin Are Death, But the Gift of God is Eternal Life! Brother McGahay was the pastor and created another **decision**: Accept the gift and never work for wages. The coin of the kingdom will be God's love, and it's free! Let's see now—I'm not only in the family, but also in the kingdom by God's spirit.*

<u>North Texas State College: First Baptist Church (Denton, Texas)</u>

Never finding the Baptist Student Union. I'm still spatially deficient although I have learned to read a map. I did find the First Baptist Church. Now, as a teenager in Breckenridge all denominations were the same to us. Whether Baptist or Methodist or Presbyterian or Catholic, we belonged where our parents chose for us, but we intermingled and were all of the family and the Kingdom. As a college student, I was called to *do a little research and make my **decision**, and that **decision** was made to link in with the Baptists as my choice!*

Young Adult: Connell Baptist Church (Fort Worth, Texas)

*So this is how church is when you have a husband and two little boys living with you: A home-to-care-for days, laundry-in-the-Bendex Washer-days, dishwashing-by-hand days, not-much-money days. The **decision** to serve God in the church becomes needful for recommitment daily, but a **decision** to be honored nevertheless.*

Mature Adult: Broadway Baptist Church (Fort Worth, Texas)

*The larger picture of this Kingdom thing: This business of Church Family. God's Kingdom and his family are not merely local entities though certainly they are local. The scope of his world and work are more far-reaching than that little girl acting the part of a Dutch girl in a blue dress wearing wooden shoes for a part in a Women's Missionary Union pageant could ever have imagined. The **decision**: Not Baptist; Not Protestant; But Christian. Jesus is God!!!*

+++++

My memories of my mom and dad and our church lives began in the early 1950s. We went to church on Sunday mornings, Sunday evenings, and Wednesday evenings. The services followed a predictable pattern: The congregation would sing a few gospel hymns and the pastor would preach a sermon. Dad would be annoyed if the Sunday morning service went longer than an hour because that meant we wouldn't beat the Methodists to the lunch line at Luby's Cafeteria.

The theology among Baptists and other conservative Christians of the day was pretty simple. The purpose of the church and its members was to bring in new converts. One converted by coming to the front of the sanctuary at the close of each service and making a public profession of faith in Jesus Christ as Lord and Savior. This was known as an altar call, even though in Baptist churches there wasn't an altar in sight. Its history, for those interested in such things, went back to Charles Finney in the 1800s with his "anxious benches". By responding to an altar call, you attained forgiveness of all sins through the shed blood of Jesus Christ and, upon your death, would be united with all the other saints in heaven. And you really needed to be baptized by immersion, although most Baptists denied that had any real salvific effect.

Beyond that, there weren't many rules Baptists had to follow. I can think of three: No dancing, no drinking alcohol, and no mixed bathing. For those confused by the term "mixed bathing", it referred to men and women (wearing bathing suits) being in a swimming pool at the same time. God forbid! Oddly, you could use tobacco products all you wanted, and the front lawn of our church was covered by a kind of blue haze before and after each service from all the smokers. When push came to shove, Baptists wanted their new converts to actually attend church and to tithe (give ten percent of their income to the church). Some people did and some didn't.

+++++

Mary lived with us in North Carolina for about 20 months before she died. She loved to cook, and the old iron skillet got plenty of use. But more than that, she loved to read. By the time she died in January 2022, the only meaningful thing left in her possession was a bookcase containing the eight cartons of books she had gathered over the 98 years of her life.

As I grieved over her death and processed the loss I felt, I realized that these books were the key to understanding who she really was, the real Mary Louise Ray Hiett. Not the mother of my childhood. Not the stay-at-home PTA mom, who fixed breakfast every morning, packed our school lunches, nagged about homework, terrorized us if we got bad grades. Not the housekeeper mom who vacuumed, cleaned the bathrooms, and made our beds. Not the caretaker mom who made sure we got to the doctor and dentist and ate fruit and vegetables now and then.

I left our home in Fort Worth for college in Denton, Texas, in June 1961 and never really came back. I got married in 1963, went to graduate school in Austin, worked in Corpus-Christi on the newspaper for a while, went into the Air Force and served a tour in Vietnam, finally ending up working on the East Coast. To my great regret, I didn't spend much time with my parents as an adult. A phone call here or there. A short visit lasting three or four days. And most of that time was spent getting caught up about all the things going on in the family. So the picture of my mother that remained frozen in my mind was completely wrong. I thought of her as being like she was when I was a kid, only older. I never realized that she had developed a completely new persona, a life all her own that didn't really involve me.

I'm a bit ashamed to admit that after her death I was taken aback at the memorial service held by her home church in Fort Worth as the pastors spoke about all her accomplishments through the years. She had started a program for the disabled. She had led a Bible study, apparently for years. She led a prayer team. She worked tirelessly on behalf of the homeless. She advocated for causes for equality and justice in the community. When did she do all that? Why didn't we ever talk about it? Who was this woman?

I finally came to understand that she had left me a clear message about who she really was. If I wanted to know her more fully, I would have to take a journey through the bookcase that was sitting in the corner of a now-empty bedroom on the second floor of our home. It would be in these books she had so carefully curated and treasured and marked up over the course of nearly a century that I would find the adult, grownup, thoughtful, caring, clever woman that I never really made the effort to get to know. My mother. This is the story of that journey.

Chapter 1
Bibles, Bibles, Bibles

———

The first thing that struck me about Mom's bookcase was the number and variety of Bibles she had accumulated and kept. By my count there were 15 of them. The Mom I remember from my growing up years only used the King James Bible, as did everyone in all the evangelical churches of the day. She had two copies of the King James Bible on her bookshelf when she died. One had belonged to her when my brother and I were children. It was marked and underlined almost from beginning to end, with notes written on every empty space throughout. That book is a monument to her faith and devotion.

Mother also kept a copy of my father's King James Bible (a gift from her, I think), and it's clear that she began to use it herself after he died in 1987. In fact, she left a meaningful quote in it which read:

> *The great truth of the resurrection is not that we have a new life after death. That is a great truth but not the greatest. This is the greatest: That we are to be new here and now, by the power of the resurrection. Not so much that we are to live forever, but that we may live more nobly today because we will live forever.*

I am unable to identify the source of the quote. I don't think it was original to Mom. It is an important clue, however, to the way her Christian faith had been changing from the simplistic and rigid doctrines I remember as a child to the more sophisticated and nuanced faith I found in her in the few months we spent together before her death.

+++++

It is impossible for Christians today to understand the extent to which the King James Version of the Bible dominated the thought and life of American evangelical Christianity up through the 1960s. Sometimes referred to as the Authorized Version, it was used exclusively in Baptist churches as well as most other Protestant denominations. Today, if we want to buy a new Bible, we have dozens and dozens of translations to choose from. And there are variations within these translations.

In contrast, the King James Bible reigned supreme throughout the English-speaking world for more than 350 years. Commissioned by King James, the son of Mary, Queen of Scots, in 1604, it was first published in 1611. It included 39 books of the Old Testament, 14 books known as the Apocrypha (generally discarded by most conservative Christians), and 27 books of the New Testament. It has long been hailed for its literary excellence and beautiful language.

When I was young (Mom would have been in her twenties and thirties), the King James Version was the only Bible we owned. It had been in use for so long that it took on a sacred quality, bordering on bibliolatry. When someone referred to the "Word of God", they didn't mean the Divine Logos (Christ Jesus). They meant the King James Version of the Holy Bible. The belief was that the King James Version was divinely inspired and inerrant, meaning each verse was literal truth and could not be questioned. I suspect that 90 percent of the Baptists we knew were not even aware that the King James Bible had been translated from Greek and Hebrew texts (not all of which agreed with each other). There was an oft-told joke in Texas which went, "If the English language was good enough for Jesus Christ, it's good enough for us."

This emphasis on the literal truth of a single translation of the Holy Bible led to a kind of doctrinal rigidity. The church had a set of beliefs (almost exclusively about salvation with virtually nothing about sanctification, that is, the spiritual process of becoming more holy in one's manner of life) and had identified Bible verses that supported those beliefs. Many Christians memorized dozens of these verses and could spout them in an argument like a gunner using a machine gun. There was little interest in understanding other ways Greek or Hebrew words might have been translated. Context mattered not at all.

In the 1950s and 1960s Mom would probably have best been characterized as a fundamentalist. Fundamentalists agreed with five key ideas: (1) The literal truth of the Bible, (2) the virgin birth and deity of Christ, (3) the substitutionary atonement of Jesus Christ on the cross, (4) the bodily resurrection of Jesus, and (5) the authenticity of Jesus' miracles as recorded in scripture. That was certainly what Mom would have been taught and believed. And the foundation on which these ideas rested was the King James Version of the Bible.

Today fundamentalism is used as a pejorative term and in our larger culture is associated with ignorance and intolerance. If you can't think of anything else bad to say about someone you disagree with, you can call him a "fundamentalist."

There was a phase commonly used in conservative Christian circles which went, "God said it; I believe it; that settles it." That phrase embodied the faith of the mother I grew up with. Clearly, over the course of the next half century, something inside her changed.

+++++

I had graduated from high school in 1961 and my brother Jack finished in 1964. After we left home for college, Mom and Dad moved their church membership from Connell Baptist Church on the west side of Fort Worth to Broadway Baptist Church, a large downtown congregation. Connell was the church Jack and I grew up in. It was a typical 1950s-style Southern Baptist church. The music consisted of traditional hymns from the Broadman Hymnal and the sermons were all essentially the same, a call to accept Jesus as savior, which 99.9 percent of us sitting there had long ago done. I would describe Connell as a kind of blue-collar Baptist church.

By contrast, Broadway was a large, urbane church with a more upscale, educated congregation. Think white collar. The pastor was Dr. J.P. Allen, and Mom loved the depth and richness of the sermons she was now hearing and the soaring hymns and chorales that filled the sanctuary with musical roots deep in the classical tradition. Mom and Dad quickly made friends in their new church home with bankers, doctors, lawyers, and professors from nearby Southwestern Baptist Theological Seminary.

The 1960s were a time of tectonic change in American culture, and Broadway Baptist Church was beginning to take that change to heart. According to a March 19, 2021, article in *Baptist News Global* written by Alan Bean, Broadway was at the forefront of a move from the simple gospel proclamation of the past to a community more engaged with its surrounding culture and community. Bean wrote:

> . . .*when Guy Moore passed the pastoral torch to Jimmy Allen in 1962, Broadway was exposed to a new take on an old gospel. A new generation of Southern Baptist scholar-pastors had been exposed to Ivy League culture, the neo-orthodox theology of Karl Barth and Reinhold Niebuhr, a surging ecumenical movement, and the non-violent direct action of Martin Luther King Jr.*

> *J.P. Allen wasn't sure how to blend these exciting new trends with the Southern piety of his youth, but he was determined to make the pieces fit. Broadway's facilities now were surrounded*

by poor neighborhoods and intractable social problems. Under Allen's leadership, the congregation responded vigorously to the need.

John Claypool introduced Broadway to confessional preaching. He didn't have all the answers and repeatedly said so. He shifted the focus from evangelical proclamation to liturgical mystery, a tradition Welton Gaddy, Claypool's successor, embraced with enthusiasm.

According to Bean, these developments made James Leo Garrett, a professor of theology at nearby Southwestern Baptist Theological Seminary, uneasy. In *Living Stones*, Garrett's history of Broadway Baptist Church, he argued that Broadway's focus had "shifted from evangelism, visitation, participative church training, Sunday school enlargement, and mission-and-church-planting" to "more liturgical worship, more emphasis on Holy Week and Advent, pastoral care and nurture of its members, and a Christian social ministry to persons and families in the community having specific needs."

Mom loved every bit of that.

+++++

It's no surprise that, as the preaching and teaching she was hearing at Broadway expanded beyond the strict limits of a more historic and rigid fundamentalism, her old King James Bible no longer fulfilled all her scriptural needs.

The first new Bible she acquired seems to have been a copy of the *Amplified Bible*. The *Amplified Bible* was conceived by a remarkable woman, Frances Siewert, who was active in Christian education and the widow of a Presbyterian minister. As noted in Wikipedia, in the early 1950s "she conceived the idea of a New Testament with 'amplifications' to more fully bring out the meaning of the original Greek words." Supported by The Lockman Foundation, she proceeded to update the style and wording of the 1901 *American Standard Version* of the Bible, incorporating glosses, explanatory phrases, and alternative renderings into the text. Her complete Old and New Testaments was published by Zondervan in 1965.

It was this 1965 version of the *Amplified Bible* that Mom acquired for her bookcase and which remained there until her death. To understand its value, we can consider a single verse, one near and dear to the hearts of all evangelicals everywhere: John 3:16. As every old Baptist knows, in the *King James Version* this reads:

> *For God so loved the world that he gave his only begotten son, that whosoever believeth in him should not perish, but have everlasting life.*

In the *Amplified Bible* this verse reads:

> *For God so greatly loved and dearly prized the world that He [even] gave up His only-begotten (unique) Son, so that whoever believes in (trusts, clings to, relies on) Him shall not perish—come to destruction, be lost—but have eternal (everlasting) life.*

To Mom, this must have seemed like a change from a black and white 15-inch television to a 21-inch color screen. I can picture her holding the two Bibles side by side, comparing her favorite verses to see the difference and to ponder the meaning of a more complex translation.

+++++

Unfortunately, while the *Amplified Bible* was good for teasing out the meaning of a particular verse, it was not a very good Bible for daily reading. The meaning of longer passages of scripture got lost in all the various translation alternatives the *Amplified Bible* offered. So Mom began acquiring other versions of the Bible as well as Bible study resources.

As life moved from the volatile 1960s into the 1970s, she seems to have acquired several new versions of the Bible, all of which were copyrighted in 1971. I assume she acquired them then or shortly thereafter. The first I will mention is a copy of *The Living Bible*, a paraphrased version of the Bible that was immensely popular for about 15 minutes. People were hungry, I think, for a version of the Bible they could read and understand. The "thee" and "thou" language of the *King James Version* was tedious and reading Paul's letters was almost impossible. But, in the end, *The Living Bible* seemed too big a change from the seriousness of the *King James Version*.

Wikipedia quotes Michael D. Marlowe, who describes himself as a Bible researcher, as criticizing *The Living Bible* as "the dumbing-down of the Biblical texts to a grade-school level". This seems fair. In retrospect, it was okay for kids but not for serious adults. Mom's copy of *The Living Bible* is unique in her collection in that she didn't have a single note in it or passage underlined anywhere.

Another Bible Mom acquired during this period was the *Revised Standard Version* (RSV). This is a serious Bible and attempted not only to update the language, but also to make use of ancient Greek texts not used by the translators of the *King James Version*. The preface notes:

> *The King James Version of the New Testament was based upon a Greek text that was marred by mistakes, containing the accumulated errors of fourteen centuries of manuscript copying. It was essentially the Greek text of the New Testament as edited by Beza, 1589, who closely followed that published by Erasmus (1516 – 1535), which was based upon a few medieval*

manuscripts. The earliest and best of the eight manuscripts which Erasmus consulted was from the tenth century, and he made the least use of it because it differed most from the commonly received text; Beza had access to two manuscripts of great value, dating from the fifth and sixth centuries, but he made very little use of them because they differed from the text published by Erasmus

We now possess many more ancient manuscripts of the New Testament and are far better equipped to seek to recover the original working of the Greek text. The evidence for the text of the books of the New Testament is better than for any other ancient book, both in the number of extant manuscripts and in the nearness of the date of some of these manuscripts to the date when the book was originally written.

Efforts to update the *King James Version* had been going on for some time, with parts of the RSV published in 1946, more in 1952, and a complete second edition in 1972. This is the copy Mom acquired. The RSV is an excellent translation and is very readable. It was widely used among mainline denominations, particularly in the Episcopal Church. But it never became popular among those whose roots were deep in the *King James Bible* culture of southern conservative Christianity. Mom seems to have used it very little. There are a few New Testament verses underlined, but it's clear she rarely used it.

A third version on Mom's bookshelf was a copy of *The Jerusalem Bible*. Published in 1971, *The Jerusalem Bible* was the first widely accepted Roman Catholic English translation of the Bible since the 17th century. It demonstrates a high level of scholarship and is sometimes used by American liberal Protestants. It is one of the versions authorized for use in the Episcopal Church.

The Jerusalem Bible is a contemporary English version of the Bible that is extremely readable. Mom seems to have used it extensively for a few years after she acquired it. The New Testament books are well marked and underlined, as was her custom. The important thing about her use of an essentially Roman Catholic version of the Bible is that she was continuing her theological journey beyond her Southern Baptist heritage with its roots in the *King James Version* of the Bible. Clearly she rejected the oft-stated belief among many Baptists that the Bishop of Rome is the anti-Christ.

At the end, however, Mom seems to have made *The New International Bible* her spiritual home. As a companion to that, she seems to have made extensive use of Eugene Peterson's *The Message*. I will share some thoughts about her use of these two versions of the Bible in Chapter 4. Before that, I want to mention some of the other texts she seemed to have acquired and used through the years.

Chapter 2
William Tyndale and Other Odd Friends

On July 12, 1994, Mom attended a lecture in the Perry Auditorium of the National Cathedral in Washington, D.C., on the Tyndale Bible, specifically on the modern-spelling edition of the 1534 *Tyndale's New Testament* prepared by David Daniell and published in 1989. She bought a copy of this Bible and left two pages of notes inside the text.

Although I knew nothing about this lecture or her interest in the background of the English Bible at the time, I do remember the occasion of this visit to Washington D.C. and the National Cathedral. After Dad's death, Mom began to organize occasional tours around the country for (mostly senior) members of Broadway Baptist Church. Apparently feeling a little guilty for coming to the D.C. area and not visiting me and my family—we were living in the area at the time—she invited Jane and me to join her and her group for a dinner she had arranged at the Watergate.

I remember this visit because of a joke she made during the meal. When the server asked if anyone wanted drinks before dinner, Mom said, "No. We're Baptists, and we don't drink in front of each other." Mother had a very acerbic sense of humor, and this joke said a lot about her journey from the literalistic and legalistic King James theology of her younger years. She clearly saw the hypocrisy of churches banning alcohol consumption publicly when most of their members drank in private. Although we grew up in a home with no alcohol, I realized later that Mom had begun to imbibe at restaurants and with friends on occasion.

The important point is that Mom was beginning to see that Christianity did not consist of a list of "do's" and "do not's". She understood that it was important to search the scriptures in their wholeness, to find the heart of the message of the Bible, and to discern God's heart as it relates to our Christian conduct. This would later become an important issue in the life of her church as it began to address issues of sexuality, something that would be extremely divisive in the church in general and Broadway in particular.

+++++

The first page of Mom's notes from the 1994 lecture on Tyndale mostly consisted of biographical information about his life. The second page listed four individuals she apparently considered particularly important to the process of developing an English version of the Bible. They include John Wycliffe (1328 – 1384), Desiderius Erasmus (1466 – 1536), William Tyndale (1494 – 1536), and Myles Coverdale (1488 – 1569). She was an astoundingly curious woman, and I have no doubt she investigated the contribution each of these made to the development of the English language Bible. I have gathered information about each of them from three sources: The introduction by David Daniell to his *Tyndale's New Testament*, *The Story of Christianity* by Justo L. Gonzalez, and various Wikipedia entries.

+++++

John Wycliffe was born in England somewhere around 1328. He became an Oxford scholar and priest who, like many others in that period, came to believe that the Roman church had become thoroughly corrupt in both its practice and doctrine. He quickly managed to annoy a lot of important people with his anti-Catholic rhetoric. Catholic authorities were particularly incensed by Wycliffe's belief that individual members of the body of Christ ought to have the scriptures available to them in their own language.

In what seems to us today to be a monumental accomplishment, he, with the assistance of several followers and friends, produced handwritten copies of the Bible in English based upon the Latin Vulgate, a version of the Bible that had been produced by Jerome, one of the early church fathers, in 384. There were, of course, revisions to the Vulgate over the years, but it was the primary version of the Bible used by the Church for the next 1,000 years. Unfortunately, the Vulgate was not a particularly good version of the Bible since it was not based on the best Greek texts. Nevertheless, it did open the door to English versions of the scriptures that could be read by ordinary believers.

Wycliffe's translation was in middle English and is completely opaque to modern readers. Some 250 copies of his version of the Bible survive today. A copy of one of these manuscripts was sold on December 5, 2016, for $1.7 million.

Wycliff died in 1384 and was buried in consecrated ground. Anger at his ideas grew within the Catholic Church over the next three decades, and he was finally condemned by the Council of Constance in 1415. Oddly, nothing was done for the next 13 years when his body was finally disinterred, his bones burned, and his ashes scattered in the river Swift. Take that, John Wycliffe.

+++++

The next character in Mom's journey through the past was Desiderius Erasmus of Rotterdam. Born in 1466, Erasmus was a scholar and priest. In 1499 he went to Oxford where he heard lectures on Paul's letters by a scholar named John Colet.

Colet, another Oxford professor and the son of the Mayor of London, in 1496 had begun to read the New Testament in Greek and translate it into English for his students at Oxford. Later, he began to read translated portions for the public at Saint Paul's Cathedral in London. This was such an astounding success that as many as 20,000 people would pack into the cathedral to hear the scriptures read in their own tongue.

Erasmus was impressed that Colet based his lectures on Greek texts rather than the traditional Latin Vulgate, and he decided to correct the Latin Vulgate using Greek texts which he was able to acquire. In 1516 Erasmus published a Greek-Latin Parallel New Testament. The Latin was not the original Vulgate, but a new version he developed using Greek New Testament manuscripts he had been able to acquire. This was the first non-Latin Vulgate to be produced in 1,000 years. It was also the first to come off a printing press. Printing using moveable type had been introduced in the mid-1400s, primarily by Johannes Gutenberg.

Erasmus was important to the development of an English Bible because he gathered and published a Greek text version of the Bible. This meant that future translators would no longer have to rely on the corrupt Latin Vulgate that was widely used throughout Christendom.

+++++

This brings us to the star of this chapter in Mom's life: William Tyndale. He was born in 1494 in a village in Gloucestershire, England. He attended Oxford and Cambridge and was considered a very learned man by all who knew him. He was fluent in eight languages. It is clear he had aligned himself with the Reformers by 1521 and in 1523 sought permission from the English Bishop Tunstall to translate the New Testament from the Greek texts into English. Tunstall declined.

According to a historical account at *greatsite.com,* Tyndale was soon forced to flee England because of the wide-spread rumor that his English New Testament project was under way. Inquisitors and bounty hunters sought to arrest him to prevent his translation project. Tyndale went to Europe and by the end of 1525 had completed a translation of the New Testament using the Greek versions of the text developed by Erasmus. The first printing was in February 1526 and copies began to arrive in England a month later. In one of the great ironies we sometimes encounter, the church authorities in England began to buy as many copies of Tyndale's Bible as they could find and burn them. This, of course, benefitted Tyndale financially and he was able to begin to translate Old Testament books as well as update his New Testament. Obviously, the authorities were unable to acquire all the copies, and many made their way into homes of Reform-minded believers throughout the country, despite the fact that it was a capital offense to even possess a copy of Tyndale's translation.

It was his 1534 edition that David Daniell updated and Mom had purchased for her collection. The John 3:16 verse we have been using as a comparison reads: *For God so loveth the world, that he hath given his only son, that none that believe in him, should perish: but should have everlasting life.*

If this sounds strangely like the same verse in the *King James Version*, it is because the scholars who eventually created the *King James Version* copied much of Tyndale's work word for word.

Tyndale was eventually betrayed by an Englishman he had befriended. He was kept in jail for 500 days before he was strangled and burned at the stake in 1536. Tyndale's last words were, *"Oh Lord, open the King of England's eyes"*.

+++++

The last name on Mom's list was that of Myles Coverdale. Coverdale was not nearly as significant as the other three, but it seems his work provided a kind of conclusion to the entire process of developing an

English Bible. Coverdale was born in 1488 in Yorkshire, England. He studied at Cambridge and entered the priesthood. He fell in with a group of Reformers but managed to escape harm by moving back and forth between England and Europe as the vagaries of the tides of Reform ebbed and flowed throughout England during the course of his life. He was an able translator and was able to complete the portions of the Old Testament Tyndale had not been able to translate before his execution. Thus Coverdale was able to publish a complete Bible containing the Old and New Testaments in 1535.

Later editions were published in 1537 and were the first complete Bibles printed in England. By this time the prohibitions against the Reformers and been removed. The 1537 edition carried the royal license and was therefore the first officially approved Bible translation in English.

Coverdale died in 1569 in England, one of the few Reformers not to be executed for his faith. While he was the first to publish a complete Bible in English, he was certainly not the last. It was not long before other translations were made leading up to the landmark King James Bible in 1611.

+++++

Mom's journey into the past did not end with this foray into the lives of William Tyndale and his friends. Never one to be satisfied with the status quo, she seems to have begun to study the Bible in its Greek and Hebrew forms.

Chapter 3
Tools of the Trade

With all the different translations of the Bible available to her, it seems clear that Mary began to wonder why they were all different. What made the translators chose one English phrase instead of another to translate what appeared to be the exact same Greek text? More importantly, which one was the more correct English translation.

She apparently began to study the Bible in its original languages. On the bookcase at her death were several interesting books. She possessed two copies of the New Testament in Greek. The first was *The Greek New Testament* published by the United Bible Societies in 1968. This book contains only the Greek version, although chapter and verse markings are present along with footnotes indicating the manuscript source. The second she seems to have acquired shortly after 1990. It was *The New Greek English Interlinear New Testament* published by Tyndale House Publishers. This was a more complete work including the Greek text, a word for word interlinear translation into English, and a parallel translation, the *New Revised Standard Version*. The NRSV is an excellent modern English translation, and one which Mom didn't otherwise possess.

As an aside, it seems worth mentioning that the collation of the Greek texts into a single document was an astoundingly daunting task, and we would be surprised if there weren't the odd disagreement here and there over a particular text. According to F.F. Bruce (*The New Testament Documents*), there are more than 5,000 Greek documents (in whole or merely fragments) extant today. The most important of these can be dated back to 350 c.e. One is the *Codex Vaticanus*, which is in the

Vatican Library in Rome. The other is the *Codex Sinaiticus*, which the British Government purchased from the Soviet Government for 100,000 pounds on Christmas Day in 1933. It is now the chief treasure of the British Museum. Two other important works are the *Codex Alexandrinus*, compiled in the fifth century, and the *Codex* Bezae, compiled in the fifth or sixth century. These currently reside in the British Museum and the Cambridge University Library, respectively. Somehow, out of all these fragments, scholars have been able to piece together a single (mostly) accepted version of the New Testament in Greek.

The Greek text by itself isn't worth much to the casual student. One needs a dictionary. Mom seems to have acquired a copy of *Young's Analytical Concordance to the Bible*. Her version was published in 1977. This concordance covers both the Old and New Testaments and includes Greek and Hebrew references. It is a ponderous book and extremely cumbersome to use, especially alongside the actual Greek or Hebrew texts. It allows one to look up any English word and find a reference to every verse in the Bible which includes that word along with the corresponding Hebrew or Greek word and the various translations it can take.

The *Young's Concordance* may have helped Mom with word studies, but it probably didn't help her much beyond that. I did find on her bookcase a copy of *Learn New Testament Greek* by John H. Dobson and *Teach Yourself Biblical Hebrew* by R.K. Harrison. The truth is, it's almost impossible to learn these languages by yourself despite what is promised on the cover to the books, and there are no notes in either book that suggest she made any headway. I did find stuck between the pages a summary of verb conjugations and noun and adjective declensions that I gave her in the 1990s. I think it was all just a bridge too far.

After the internet became widely used (and she used the internet a lot, even up to her death at 98), I suspect she became adept at finding translations online, a much more useful option. I recall her asking me about it, and I referred her to a couple of my favorite websites for translating Greek and Hebrew terms and phrases.

+++++

She also had acquired a copy of the Jewish Publication Society *Hebrew-English Tanakh*, published in 1999. This is an elegant book and would have cost her dearly at a time when her resources were meager. It shows how much she valued books, even ones she couldn't actually read. The Tanakh is the Jewish version of the Christian Old Testament. Its name is a kind of anagram. The *T* refers to the word *torah*, the five books of Moses. The *N* refers to the *nevi'im*, the prophets. The *K* refers to the *kethuvim*, the writings.

The JPS version of the Hebrew scriptures is based upon what is referred to as the Masoretic text. This text is the authoritative Hebrew text of the 24 books of the Tanakh. According to notes in Wikipedia, it was collated by a group of Jews known as Masoretes between the seventh and tenth centuries (c.e.). The development of this version of the Hebrew scriptures was necessary because there were multiple versions of these documents, and they did not all agree. The creation of the Masoretic text resulted in a single, unified version generally agreed to by most Jewish groups. This version of the Hebrew scriptures is the basis for most Protestant translations of the Old Testament, including the *King James Version*, the *New American Standard Version*, and the *New International Version*. Since 1943, it has been used for Catholic Bibles as well.

+++++

The Hebrew text is difficult for the layperson to use. The alphabet is completely different from English and is written from right to left. While Mom could do word studies in Greek with the resources available to her, the Hebrew was beyond her capabilities. When she complained to me once about that, I gave her a copy of the *Septuagint*, a version of the Old Testament in Greek, which she retained until her death. I'm pretty sure she never actually used it, but she did value it.

According to legend, the Hebrew Torah (the first five books of the Old Testament) was translated into Greek by 70 Jewish scholars somewhere between 285 and 247 b.c.e. These scholars, according to the legend, miraculously produced exact renderings in Greek from the available Hebrew texts. This story seemed designed to encourage belief in the authenticity of the Greek version. Because there were 70 scholars, the version they produced is referred to as LXX or the *Septuagint*. The remainder of the Hebrew scriptures were translated over the next couple of centuries.

The *Septuagint* was important because Greek had become the *lingua franca* throughout the Mediterranean world, including the Near East. Even in Israel, Hebrew was disappearing. By the time of Jesus in the first century, Aramaic was the common language. Even Jews were regularly using the *Septuagint*. As the Christian writings were created (eventually the New Testament), quotations from the Jewish scriptures were taken primarily, although not exclusively, from the *Septuagint* rather than being translated from the Hebrew.

As Christianity spread and the divide with Judaism became greater and greater, the Jews saw the need to reconnect with their scriptures in the ancient Hebrew form. As noted previously, this led to the development of the Masoretic text used in the Jewish community today.

+++++

In addition to her Greek and Hebrew texts, Mom acquired commentaries—a lot of them. The one I want to mention first is *The Jerome Biblical Commentary*, published in 1968 by Prentice-Hall and edited by Raymond E. Brown, Joseph A. Fitzmyer, and Roland E. Murphy. What is particularly interesting about this book is that it is a Roman Catholic work, dedicated to the memory of Pope Pius XII. This seems an odd choice for a Baptist like Mom, but my personal experience has been that Catholic Bible scholars are excellent because they comment within the bounds of historic Christian doctrine. Liberal Protestant scholars are prone to flights of fancy and allow their comments to go beyond the traditional bounds of Christian propriety.

Mom also had three volumes of *The New International Commentary on the New Testament*. Published by William B. Eerdmans Publishing at various intervals beginning in 1951, the commentary was edited initially by F.F. Bruce and later by Gordon D. Fee, both well-known Bible scholars. Mom possessed three of these volumes: *The Gospel of Luke* by Norval Geldenhuys, *The Book of the Acts (Revised)* by F.F. Bruce, and *The Gospel of Mark* by William L. Lane.

She possessed a second commentary on the book of Acts, *The Communicator's Commentary: Acts* by Lloyd J. Ogilvie. Rev. Ogilvie served as Chaplain of the U.S. Senate from 1995 through 2003. He had previously served in various pastorates, including more than 20 years as pastor of First Presbyterian Church of Hollywood. His is the only commentary in Mom's collection written by a pastor rather than an academic.

She possessed two commentaries on the Book of Hebrews. The first was *The Message of Hebrews* by Raymond Brown; the second was *Understanding the Book of Hebrews* by Robert L. Cargill.

There were two books on the Psalms in her collection. Although not strictly commentaries, they would have been useful to her in her own reading and as a Bible teacher. The first was *The Case for the Psalms* by Anglican theologian N.T. Wright. The second was Rabbi Harold S. Kushner's *The Lord Is My Shepherd.* There was a commentary on the Old Testament Book of Isaiah by Trent C. Butler, and a commentary on the ten commandments by William Barclay.

The final book I would mention from her collection is *The Revell Bible Dictionary* edited by Lawrence O. Richards and published by the Fleming H. Revell Company in 1990. This is a wonderful single-volume illustrated dictionary that would have allowed Mom to learn in more detail just about anything related to names and places in the Bible. Oddly, she had two passages marked in this dictionary with sticky notes. One was for Rahab and the other was Tamar, both of whom engaged in prostitution. Wonder what mother was thinking?

+++++

Mary was not a casual reader of anything, especially something as important as the Bible. Her exposure to a wide variety of English versions of the Bible seems to have led her into study of the Greek and Hebrew texts upon which the English translations rested. Her use of the original texts seems to have been primarily for word studies rather than any deeper theological purpose. She supplemented her Bible study with a Bible dictionary and a variety of commentaries. I know of seminary graduates who have fewer resources available to them.

Chapter 4
A Couple of More Bibles

On Friday evening, January 28, 2022, Mom fell onto the floor of her bedroom in a coma. She never regained consciousness and died in the hospital 36 hours later. The cause of death was thyroid disease, a condition that had not been previously diagnosed. As I have been going through the Bibles she left behind, I finally came to the one she used regularly for the last 30 years of her life. It was a copy of the *New International Version* of the Bible, published by Zondervan in 1988. A gift from one of her children, she cherished it and read it daily for the rest of her life.

Mom used her Bibles a little like filing cabinets. It was stuffed full of torn off pieces of paper and backs of envelopes with notes that she had taken from sermons or Bible teachings. Its pages had underlining and circles and boxes from beginning to end. Blank pages were filled with the ideas she thought important. I was especially moved to see that the last page she read before she began the journey from this life to the next was I Corinthians 13. This is a well-known passage, often read even at secular weddings. I think it worth citing here:

> *And now I will show you the most excellent way. If I speak in the tongues of men and of angels, but have not love, I am only a resounding gong or a clanging cymbal. If I have the gift of prophecy and can fathom all mysteries and all knowledge, and if I have a faith that can move mountains, but have not love, I am nothing. If I give all I possess to the poor and surrender my body to the flames, but have not love, I gain nothing.*

Love is patient, love is kind. It does not envy, it does not boast, it is not proud. It is not rude, it is not self-seeking, it is not easily angered, it keeps no record of wrongs. Love does not delight in evil but rejoices with the truth. It always protects, always trusts, always hopes, always perseveres.

Love never fails. But where there are prophecies, they will cease; where there are tongues, they will be stilled; where there is knowledge, it will pass away. For we know in part and we prophesy in part, but when perfection comes, the imperfect disappears. When I was a child, I talked like a child, I thought like a child, I reasoned like a child. When I became a man, I put childish ways behind me. Now we see but a poor reflection as in a mirror; then we shall see face to face. Now I know in part; then I shall know fully, even as I am fully known.

And now these three remain: faith, hope and love. But the greatest of these is love. (NIV)

It has been comforting to our family to know that the last chapter she saw from her beloved Bible was this famous passage from Paul on love.

+++++

The *New International Version* of the Bible was first published in 1978 by Biblica, formerly the International Bible Society (Wikipedia). The idea behind a new translation began in 1955 when an evangelical engineer and businessman named Howard Long became convinced that it was simply too difficult to communicate the gospel using a 300-year-old version of the English Bible. Long shared his frustration with his pastor, and they approached their denomination, the Christian Reformed Church (CRC), about the need for a new English version of the Bible. The CRC formed a committee in 1957 to assess the need for a new Bible. In 1964 a joint committee of the CRC and the National Association of Evangelicals issued invitations to a translation conference which met in August 1965 at Trinity Christian College in Palos Heights, Illinois. The decision was made to begin work on a new Bible.

In 1967, the New York Bible Society (later called Biblica[1]) took responsibility for the project and hired a team of Evangelical scholars to complete the work. The New Testament was published in 1973 and the complete Bible in 1978. Since then, the NIV has become one of the top-selling bibles with more than 450 million sold worldwide.

+++++

The first thing I noticed as I looked through Mom's NIV Bible is that she had written the Apostles' Creed just inside the front cover. This alone stands in stark contrast to the King James Mary of my youth. In the Baptist Church we didn't even know what creeds were, let alone recite them. I remember as a teenager attending the Methodist Church of my girlfriend (now my wife Jane) and being shocked when they all stood up and recited the Apostles' Creed. I didn't know if it was a demonic cult thing, and I refused to recite it for a year or so. I eventually concluded that there was nothing heretical about it (with the possible exception of the "he descended into hell" part).

The creed itself reads as follows:

> *I believe in God the Father Almighty, the maker of heaven and earth, and in Jesus Christ, His only Son, our Lord, who was conceived by the Holy Spirit, born of the Virgin Mary, suffered under Pontius Pilate, was crucified, dead and buried. He descended into hell. The third day he arose again from the dead, ascended into heaven, and sits at the right hand of the*

---

1. https://en.wikipedia.org/wiki/Biblica

Father Almighty; from thence he shall come to judge the quick and the dead.

I believe in the Holy Spirit; the holy Catholic church, the communion of the saints, the forgiveness of sins, the resurrection of the body and life everlasting. Amen.

There are two important creeds used in the Church today. Probably the more important is the Nicene Creed. As Christianity developed over the first three centuries, it became clear that there existed within the church diverse ideas about key doctrinal elements. Because of these differences, the various factions within the Church were finding it increasingly difficult to get along. The Emperor Constantine, who intended for the Christian Church to be a unifying element in the Roman world, called a council together in 325 c.e. at Nicea, an ancient city in Greece, to resolve these disputes. To call the meeting contentious would be an understatement. Nevertheless, a large enough contingent managed to reach agreement and the Nicene Creed was the outcome. The losers sulked off and immediately began planning their revenge. Over time, it became clear that there were still some lack of clarity in the creed and a second council was held at Constantinople in 381. This resulted in the creed as it exists today.

The Niceno-Constantinopolitan Creed has remained in use for more than 1600 years. It is the primary creed used in the Roman and Eastern churches and the Anglican churches throughout the world.

The other creed is the Apostles' Creed. The history of this creed is less clear than for the Nicene Creed, and elements can be traced back to an ancient Roman baptismal creed. The text as used today seems to have developed in southern Gaul around 450 c.e. The Apostles' Creed is commonly used today in the historic mainline denominations such as Methodists, Presbyterians, Lutherans, and others. The Anglicans use it during baptisms but keep to the Nicene Creed for Eucharist (communion) services.

Why did Mary, after a life of faith as a Baptist of more than 60 years, suddenly decide to inscribe the Apostles' Creed in her Bible. There are, I think, several reasons. First, the church she was attending, Broadway Baptist Church, had begun to introduce historic liturgical elements into its Sunday worship. Second, as we will see in later chapters, she began to study the history of the Church as it developed in the West. This would have given her a clear understanding of the importance of the various creeds developed over the past two millennia. Third, she began to be much more ecumenical in her thinking. In particular, she began to read authors who were Catholic and Jewish in their faith life.

This last point is attested to by a quote she had written in the back inside cover of her NIV Bible. It is from Pope John 23rd: " See everything; overlook a lot; change a little."

+++++

I cannot begin to describe all the notes and underlining in this Bible. However, there are some handwritten notes and references to scripture verses on scraps of paper stuck between the pages that are worth mentioning. In Chapter 1 I noted that Mom had written in Dad's King James Bible (which she used herself after his death until she got her NIV Bible) a brief comment beginning "The great truth of the resurrection. . . ." This was clearly something of deep meaning to her because she inscribed it again in her NIV Bible.

Some of the scripture references she included were:

> *Habakkuk 3:17,18. Though the fig tree does not bud and there are no grapes on the vines, though the olive crop fails, and the fields produce no food, though there are no sheep in the pen and*

no cattle in the stalls, yet I will rejoice in the Lord, I will be joyful in God my Savior.

Hebrews 10:36. You need to persevere so that when you have done the will of God, you will receive what he has promised.

Ecclesiastes 3:15. He has made everything beautiful in its time. He has also set eternity in the hearts of men; yet they cannot fathom what God has done from beginning to end.

Mark 12:28-34. One of the teachers of the law came and heard them debating. Noticing that Jesus had given them a good answer he asked him, "Of all the commandments, which is the most important?"

"The most important one," answered Jesus, "is this: 'Hear, O Israel, the Lord our God, the Lord is one. Love the Lord your God with all your heart and with all our soul and with all your mind and with all your strength.' The second is this. 'Love your neighbor as yourself.' There is no commandment greater than these."

"Well said, teacher," the man replied. "You are right in saying that God is one and there is no other but him. To love him with all your heart, with all your understanding and with all your strength, and to love your neighbor as yourself is more important than all burnt offerings and sacrifices,"

When Jesus saw that he had answered wisely, he said to him, "You are not far from the kingdom of God." And from then on no one dared ask him any more questions.

It is clear from these few passages that Mom had moved beyond the legalism that had been central to her Baptist faith when she was much younger. She was beginning to search out the heart of the Christian faith. She had come to understand with the passing of the years and the losses we invariably suffer that we still worship God joyfully because of who He is, not because of what He does for us. She also understood that we live life in the present, but with an awareness that God always has in mind a future for us. And she understood that, while we await that future, we need to continue loving God, carrying his love to all our neighbors in practical ways.

On another scrap of paper in her NIV Bible was a reference to an article published by her friend Dr. Jim Dennison. It was a quote made by a female of the Sufi religion who lived in the eighth century named Rabia, which read, *"In my soul there is a temple, a shrine, a mosque, a church where I kneel. Prayer should bring us to an altar where no walls or names exist."* Mom then added the quote from Matthew 23:19 where Jesus asks, *"Which is greater, the gift or the altar that makes the gift sacred?"*

Mom was not a universalist, but she had a profound respect for people of other faiths and grasped truth wherever it could be found.

+++++

Mom had three other Bibles on her bookshelf. One was the "Serendipity" version of the NIV, and two were different versions of *The Message* by pastor and translator Eugene Peterson. She seems to never have used any of these. There are no markings in them at all. They were perhaps gifts. We'll never know.

Chapter 5
The Meaning of the Bible

Mary loved poetry, a trait I sadly do not share. In 2014 she wrote a poem that included the following lines:

I love Truth, Absolutes:

The fact that some things are irrefutable

And that God's laws dominate.

Though man messes up much in this world—and we do mess up,

Yet the earth will turn on its axis and the sun will rise again,

Perhaps unseen behind a weeping cloud; but it will rise.

The tides are Absolute; outside the province of man's messing.

The wind blows where it will.

Human life is finite!

There are Absolutes.

And while God's laws are dominant, so is his love.

I love it that God is love—and grace.

And that is Absolute.

As soon as we were old enough to understand anything, we understood Mom's expectations. She believed in right over wrong; ethical over unethical; moral over immoral. She had little patience for those who tried to skirt the line between right and wrong. To her there was no gray area. The means never justified the ends.

+++++

Even though she had come over the years to think beyond the literal words of scripture, especially in its King James form, she also believed scripture leads to a truth, an absolute that we need to seek out and find and use in our daily lives.

As a child I saw a drawing intended to depict how God gave us the scriptures as we have them today. In the drawing there was an ethereal bearded white-haired old man (God), sort of floating overhead, whispering in the ear of a scribe who was writing down the words of the Bible, taking dictation, as it were. This is a powerful image and gives a sacred quality to every single word of scripture. This, I think, fairly describes our understanding of the Bible in those days. We assumed that the *King James Version*, which had been in use for nearly 350 years, was literally true and to be taken word for word.

Mom certainly started out with that view of scripture, but her journey took her well beyond it. We can follow her on her faith journey through the Bibles and Bible tools she lovingly collected over the years. She began by gathering a variety of English translations of the Bible, contrasting and comparing the language they used to communicate the Bible's central ideas. She studied the Greek and Hebrew words that were the foundation for these translations. She gathered commentaries by scholars from a variety of Christian traditions, both Catholic and Protestant.

In seeking out the richer meaning of the texts, she never abandoned the belief that there was an absolute truth to be found through the study of scriptures. This is very different from those who reject some or all the Jewish and Christian writings because there are inconsistencies or historical inaccuracies (although there are fewer of these than some would like us to believe). The story of Abraham taking Isaac up the mountain ostensibly to sacrifice him may be hard to accept as a literally accurate account. But it does contain truth about who God is and who we are in relation to Him and what His call on our lives really entails. Real truth is where you find it, and Mom understood that there was real truth to be found in every nook and cranny of the Bible.

+++++

During her last months Mom and I discussed a lot of Biblical and theological issues. One of the topics was the creation story. She was well aware that the creation story could not be literally true. A good example would be the mark God gave to Cain so that no one would kill him. Who exactly would that have been? So far as the Bible goes, there were only three people left: Adam, Eve, and Cain. Where did all these other people come from? The Bible doesn't say. That's because the point of the whole story was God's divine protection on the murderer Cain, in spite of the fact that he killed Abel. It's a story of God's mercy and grace.

+++++

We tend to treat the Bible as a stand-alone book, a single volume. That is not what it is. It is a collection of documents written by different people in different circumstances to different audiences over hundreds of years and carefully curated by Jewish scholars and Christian leaders into the single volume we have today. It includes poetry, narrative accounts initially passed down orally and later put into written form, histories, genealogies, rules and regulations, letters, apocalyptic writings, and proverbial sayings. Some of this was never intended to be understood literally, the Song of Songs, for example. Some of it, however, was intended to be taken as historically accurate. In all of it, there is to be found what Mom called the Absolute, a truth to guide us in our faith journey.

+++++

There are a variety of approaches to the interpretation of scripture (sometimes referred to as hermeneutical principles). During the first three or four centuries of Christianity, the church fathers often treated difficult passages as allegory. They said that elements of a story or section of scripture (sometimes called a pericope) symbolized some deeper, spiritual reality. While generally rejected by modern Protestants, the use of allegory is not completely far-fetched. Some of Jesus' parables were clearly intended to be allegories (the sower and the seed). Paul occasionally used analogies. The apocalyptic writings (the Book of Revelation and part of Daniel) are clearly allegory. But the allegories were often taken too far and sometimes seem unhinged theologically and doctrinally.

The reaction to this was the trend toward literalism, strictly limiting the interpretation of a passage to the words of the text. The literal interpretation of scripture is something Mom grew up with and something I was taught as a young Baptist in the 1950s and 1960s. Many people hold to this today, and I don't want to leave the impression that there is anything wrong with that. We each have our own journey. Mom and I discussed this at length in the last couple of years of her life, and it's clear that she had moved beyond that.

+++++

One of the books Mom possessed was *Zealot: The Life and Times of Jesus of Nazareth* by Reza Aslan. In the Author's Note at the beginning of the book Aslan wrote:

> *The bedrock of evangelical Christianity, at least as it was taught to me, is the unconditional belief that every word of the Bible is God-breathed and true, literal and inerrant. The sudden realization that this belief is patently and irrefutably false, that the Bible is replete with the most blatant and obvious errors and contradiction—just as one would expect from a document written by hundreds of hands across thousands of years—left me confused and spiritually unmoored. And so, like many people in my situation, I angrily discarded my faith as if it were a costly forgery I had been duped into buying. I began to rethink the faith and culture of my forefathers, finding in them as an adult a deeper, more intimate familiarity than I ever had as a child, the kind that comes from reconnecting with an old friend after many years apart.*

Aslan's family were from the Middle East and, according to his Wikipedia page, he is currently a practicing Muslim. Bart D. Ehrman, chair of the Department of Religious Studies at the University of North Carolina at Chapel Hill, tells almost exactly the same story from his own life in his book *Misquoting Jesus*. He was raised in a fundamentalist Christian environment and believed in the literal truth of scripture. When at university he discovered that there were contradictions and discrepancies in some of the historical accounts in the Bible, he lost his Christian faith.

While these accounts are sad, they also seem a tad pathetic. Mom was, by her own account, a practicing Christian for more than 90 years. Over that time she moved from a literalistic understanding of scripture to one that saw the great truths to which the Biblical narratives pointed. She absolutely believed that the weight of the creation stories, full of contradictions though they may be, pointed to a Creator in whom she could believe and whom she could worship. She believed absolutely that the resurrection stories of the New Testament were not salvific in themselves, but the truth behind them—the life, death, and bodily resurrection of Jesus—was. Mom was not a Christian because she believed in the Bible, she was a Christian because she believed in the greater realities to which the Bible points.

+++++

The 19th century gave rise to what is referred to as Biblical criticism. This was an attempt to critique texts of scripture objectively using a variety of tools developed for such a purpose. Biblical criticism includes historical criticism, form criticism, source criticism, and others. These can be excellent techniques for the study of the Bible and are widely used by scholars today.

Unfortunately, many of those who used such approaches fell under the sway of Friedrich Schleiermacher. Schleiermacher was a theologian who lived from 1768 to 1834. He moved away from a literal interpretation of the Bible, believing that its connection to "how we feel about it" was much more important. (I understand that is an oversimplification). Schleiermacher is known today as the father of liberal Protestantism. He and those who came after him considered scripture as nice stories and good ideas, but sometimes laughed when people tried to treat them as actual historical events.

+++++

If I may insert here a story of my own, I can give an example of this from my own life. Many years ago my wife and I attended a historic Presbyterian Church in downtown Washington D.C. One of the pastors was leading a Bible study and a participant made a comment about Jesus' resurrection. To the shock of all of us, the pastor interjected, "You don't mean you believe Jesus was actually resurrected in his body?" I can't begin to list all the things wrong with that pastor's comment, not least of which was its arrogance and rudeness.

A pastor of a large Methodist congregation near Mom's home church in Fort Worth was preaching on the passage where Jesus walked on water. His comment was that, "If Jesus walked on water, it was because he knew where the rocks were." I had a seminary professor say that the miracle of Jesus' feeding the 5,000 was that people simply opened their packs and passed around their extra food.

This is not the place to delineate all the damage done by poor use of Biblical criticism coupled with an over-the-top liberal theology. This is certainly not the approach Mom took in her own study of the Bible.

+++++

Biblical criticism, however, can be used to help us understand the contradictions and confusions we find in scripture with an eye toward growing our faith in its underlying truths. We might think of this as positive Biblical criticism. It is a use of the Bible in a way that builds faith rather than tears it down. I think immediately of Bishop N.T. Wright, an Anglican Bible scholar and theologian who has written prolifically within the confines of historic orthodox Christianity.

+++++

As I visited with Mom daily over the last two years of her life, I came to understand something of how she interpreted scripture. That is, I understood something of her hermeneutical principal.

I believe there were five principles that she followed. We have a clue to one of them in the fact that she inscribed the Apostles' Creed inside her Bible. It is helpful to interpret the different parts of the Bible in light of the fundamental truths laid out in this creed: The trinity, the deity of Christ, the holy spirit, the church, the resurrection (of Jesus and of us in the future). She accepted those as truth and interpreted scripture accordingly.

Another principal she followed was to consider each individual passage in light of the whole of scripture. The occasional harshness of the Old Testament God melts away when we consider the love, forgiveness, mercy, and grace as shown in other passages of both the Old and the New Testaments. Because she spent so much time studying the Bible, she did not fall prey to the mistake of building her theology around a single passage.

As will be discussed in future chapters, she had a very strong view of the role of the church, both local, historic, and universal. During the middle ages the monolithic Roman Church engaged in horrific excesses and justified many of those excesses with a very selective and incorrect reading of scripture. There is something to be said for having a church diverse not only in its membership but also in the way each expresses the common faith. This creates a marketplace of ideas about the meaning of various passages of scripture, open to consideration by all. I can affirm without question that Mom loved the church and allowed her understanding of scripture to be informed by the important place God's church held in her heart and mind.

She interpreted scripture in light of her own experiences of life. She understood the pain of life. She frequently spoke to me of her father's suicide, the struggles of her family during the depression, the difficulties of getting along with family and friends over the years, the pain of the sickness and death of her husband, and loss of companionship as her life-long friends passed away one by one. The *pathos* one finds in scripture meant a lot to her in her final years.

I have implied that Mom rejected liberal Protestantism. That is not quite true. She rejected the efforts by some to deconstruct fundamental Christian ideas, leaving us with a Rotary Club kind of communal life. She passionately accepted the call of what is sometime referred to as the social gospel—the necessity of meeting the real life needs of the less fortunate in our communities for food, clothes, shelter and love and acceptance. But she never waned in her belief that these efforts were always done in the context of the Absolutes of the historic doctrines of the Church illuminated by the texts of the Bible she loved so dearly.

And, finally, Mom believed in a future life in the presence of the King of Glory she had worshipped and followed for nearly a century. When she read the Bible in her last years, and she read it every day, she saw in it a profound hope for the future, not just in this life, but the next. She affirmed to me many times in those last days that she did not fear death. She had run her race and was ready to leave this life for the one that would come after. Every time she read a passage of scripture in those last days, she read hope into it, not just hope for her own future, but hope for the future of those she loved that she would be leaving behind.

Mom died with the following Franciscan Benediction on a bookmark in her Bible. It reads:

May God bless you with

discomfort at easy answers,

half-truths, and superficial

relationships so that you may

live deep within your heart.

May God bless your anger at

injustice, oppression and

exploitation of people so that

you may work for justice,

freedom and peace.

May God bless you with tears

to shed for those who suffer

pain, rejection, hunger and

war so that you may reach out

your hand to comfort them

and to turn their pain into Joy.

And may God bless you with

enough foolishness to believe

that you can make

a difference in the world so that

you can do what others claim

cannot be done to bring

justice and kindness to all our

children.

Amen.

Chapter 6
Mary and Her Church

In the 1950s and 1960s our family attended Connell Baptist Church on the west side of Fort Worth, Texas. Connell was a traditional Southern Baptist Church with a Sunday attendance of about 200 people. The church offered Sunday School, Sunday morning worship services, Sunday evening Training Union, Sunday evening worship services, and Wednesday evening prayer services. Television (especially the Dallas Cowboys) eventually shut down almost everything except Sunday morning activities and the youth group. We attended all of it except for Training Union, which, as far as I know, no one attended.

There was a lot of pressure on members to invite guests. This was the entire growth strategy. The only outreach activity I can think of was the church's participation in the softball league. Dad loved softball and we went to a lot of games. Church members were always on the lookout for some ringers to add to the team. The only catch was, they couldn't play on the team without joining the church. So each spring we had a couple of burly young men making a profession of faith and joining the church. Once the season was over, so was their faith journey. We wished them well.

In all the years I attended Connell, I never heard a sermon calling for us to serve the poor or care for the needy. Most sermons were of the sort that said, "Stop sinning or you'll go to hell, unless you know Jesus, which makes everything okay, but you probably should stop sinning anyway." Like most Baptist churches of the day, Connell was all about serving its own members. It was truly a church without a vision.

By the time my brother and I left home, Mom had had enough. She and Dad transferred their membership to a large downtown church, Broadway Baptist, that was liturgical, inspirational, and aspirational. I don't know if they had a softball team. But they did care about social justice, racial justice, poverty, the homeless, the disabled, the elderly. And they put their time and talents toward issues outside the four walls of the sanctuary. Mom fell in love with all of that. And she began to change.

Over the years Mom came to believe that all churches are linked together by a common history. Her view was that every individual church was related to others in its community and churches throughout the world by their common heritage. She explored this idea through her study of church history. There were four books on her bookcase that shaped her thought about the church and showed her love of the church both historic and universal.

+++++

The Church History by Eusebius (translated by Paul L. Maier)

Eusebius was born around 260 c.e., probably in Caesarea Maritime, a city on the Mediterranean coast in what would now be northern Israel. Caesarea was an early Christian center and played an important role in many of the travels noted in the New Testament Book of Acts. Origen lived and wrote in Caesarea in the third century. Along with Pamphilus of Caesarea, Origen founded an extensive library containing more than 30,000 manuscripts (later lost).

In his early years Eusebius was a student of Pamphilus, Bishop of Caesarea. Because of this, he was acquainted with the vast library that had been gathered there. Eusebius was a prolific writer and many of his works are available today. The most important of these is his history of the church, which he began working on just prior to the year 300 and completed before 325 c.e.

Of critical importance are the sources that Eusebius used in the preparation of his history. In addition to his use of the New Testament and the Hebrew scriptures, Eusebius cites such ancient writers as Hegesippus, Justin, Irenaeus, Dionysius of Alexandria, Tertullian, and Papias.

In this work Eusebius left us a great treasure since he quotes works of early witnesses whose writings would otherwise be lost to us. Of particular interest is the legacy of Papias, who lived from 60 to 130 c.e. Papias was Bishop of Hieropolis, the site of a church in what is now Turkey founded under Paul's influence (probably when he was at Ephesus). It is believed that Philip (the deacon appointed along with Stephen and five others in the Book of Acts) spent the last years of his life there. Philip's daughters were said to have acted as prophetesses in the region.

Papias personally knew a person he referred to as John the Elder (presbyter). This gets us into something of a quagmire because most people today assume there was one John among the followers of Jesus. But it was a common name and there certainly could have been more than one. Whichever John this was, Papias considered him to be one of the eyewitnesses to the founding Christian events.

Papias was also a companion of Polycarp, Bishop of Smyrna and an early Christian martyr. He was born in 69 and executed in 155. Polycarp was one of three chief Apostolic Fathers, along with Clement of Rome and Ignatius of Antioch. Polycarp also knew John as a mentor and was personally installed by John as the Bishop in Smyrna. Both Papias and Polycarp knew the daughters of Philip who themselves had known the original apostles.

Papias wrote an "Exposition of the Sayings of the Lord" somewhere around 100 c.e. The work is now completely lost except for passages quoted by Origen (180 c.e.) and Eusebius in his history. Eusebius also used Josephus and Philo as sources. Interestingly, Mom had a copy of the works of both Josephus and Philo on her bookcase. Josephus' writings are particularly interesting to Christians because he tells of events contemporary to the times of Jesus and the early church. He was something of a scoundrel and his writings can't always be taken at face value. Philo of Alexandria was a Hellenistic Jewish philosopher who lived in Alexandria in Egypt. He was born in 20 b.c.e. and died in 50 c.e. He is notable for his attempts to use allegory to harmonize Jewish scripture (Torah) with Greek philosophy. Mom certainly read Josephus, but Philo's work is difficult and there are no notes or markings to indicate she read it.

Eusbius states in the opening of his history that it was his purpose to record:

> *The successions from the holy apostles and the periods extending from our Savior's time to our own;*
>
> *The many important events that occurred in the history of the church;*
>
> *Those who were distinguished in its leadership at the most famous locations;*
>
> *Those who in each generation proclaimed the Word of God by speech or pen;*
>
> *The names, number, and ages of those who, driven by love of novelty to the extremity of error, have announced themselves as sources of knowledge (falsely so-called) while ravaging Christ's flock mercilessly, like ferocious wolves;*

The fate that overtook the whole Jewish race after their plot against our Savior;

The occasions and times of the hostilities waged by heathens against the divine Word and the heroism of those who fought to defend it, sometimes through torture and blood;

The martyrdoms of our own time and the gracious deliverance provided by our Savior and Lord, Jesus the Christ of God, who is my starting point.

Eusebius then proceeded to present his history organized into 10 sections (which he called books). These were:

The Person and Work of Christ

The Apostles

Missions and Persecutions

Bishops, Writings, and Martyrdoms

Western Heroes, Eastern Heretics

Origen and Atrocities at Alexandria

Dionysius and Dissent

The Great Persecution

The Great Deliverance

Constantine and Peace

Eusebius ends his history just before the Council of Nicaea which resulted in the great creed used throughout Christendom for the next 1700 years. Eusebius was a key figure in the council and was personally acquainted with the Emperor Constantine. Every Christian should read Eusebius' history because it provides an important understanding of the foundational events that occurred at the close of the Christian canon. In it he describes heroes of the faith during those years along with the controversies that beset the church.

+++++

Eusebius' history helped expand Mom's views regarding the church universal. Instead of focusing only on our own local churches, Eusebius invites us to see the spread of Christ's Church in a kind of messy way, in fits and starts. Some churches thrive; others struggle. There are good shepherds and incompetent ones. Even the most devoted Christians don't always get along. And yet in those early days the good news spread far and wide, across the near East, into Egypt and North Africa, through Turkey and as far west as Spain.

Eusebius also gives us a new perspective on the events in Palestine during the time of Jesus. He points us back once more to the early eyewitnesses of Jesus' life, death, and resurrection. If we are troubled by modern criticisms of the truths of the gospel accounts, Eusebius reminds us that there are witnesses whose voices we can still hear in the extra-canonical writings of the early bishops and the Church Fathers.

Mom's encounter with Eusebius would have been a reminder to her that there is more to the Christian faith than what happens within the four walls of whichever local congregation we call home. It is our common history, deeply rooted in the first and second centuries of the faith, that connect us to churches across the globe.

+++++

The Story of Christianity (**Volumes 1 and 2**) **by Justo L. Gonzalez**

This is a seminal work and belongs in every Christian's library. It is extremely readable, despite the fact that it covers a lot of very complex topics. The author, Justo L. Gonzalez, was a Cuban-born theologian, historian, and author. Born in Havana in 1929, he immigrated to the United States in 1960. He received his Bachelor of Divinity from Union Theological Seminary in New York City and his doctorate from Vanderbilt University. Gonzalez was a prolific author and wrote more than 40 books on Christian theology, history, and practice. Gonzalez was a professor of history and theology at Columbia Theological Seminary in Decatur, GA, and he served as the president of the American Society of Church History. He died in 2020 at the age of 91.

The Story of Christianity was first published in 1984 in two volumes. It is a comprehensive overview of Christian history from the time of Jesus up to beginning of the third millennium and has sold more than 1 million copies worldwide.

Volume 1 of the book covers the history of Christianity from the time of Jesus up to the Reformation. It describes important events such as the Crucifixion of Jesus, the life and ministry of Paul, the Council of Nicaea, the Great Schism between the Eastern and Western churches, the rise of the Roman Catholic Church, the Protestant Reformation, and the Counter-Reformation. The book also covers important doctrinal topics such as the nature of God, the Trinity, divine grace, and the role of the Bible in Christian faith and practice. Gonzalez also covers the doctrines of the church and the early councils in the fourth and fifth centuries. These include the differences between Arianism and Trinitarianism, the development of the Nicene Creed, the Council of Ephesus and the doctrine of the hypostatic union, and the Council of Chalcedon and the two natures of Christ.

In Volume 2 Gonzalez covers the history of Christianity from the Reformation to the present day. He describes important events such as the rise of religious movements within Protestantism (e.g., Calvinism, Anabaptism, and Anglicanism), the Age of Enlightenment and the birth of modern science, the missionary movement, the rise of Pentecostalism, and the emergence of the ecumenical movement. The book also covers important theological topics such as the nature of salvation, the role of women in the church, and the relationship between faith and culture.

+++++

Mom would have been particularly interested in what Gonzalez had to say about the organization of the church in the first and second centuries. These include the structure of the church hierarchy, the role of bishops, the relationship between local and universal churches, the development of the episcopal system, and the practice of the Eucharist (Communion).

Mom would have also been interested in the discussion of the rise of monasticism as a reaction to what many believed was the cooptation of Christianity by the Roman authorities for political purposes. Gonzalez also describes the role of asceticism in Christian spirituality, the development of organized religious orders, the influence of Eastern monasticism on Western Christianity, and the impact of monasticism on the wider society.

But most of all, Mom would have been fascinated by the events surrounding the development of the key doctrines of the church as these were worked out in the Council of Nicaea, the Council of Constantinople, the Council of Chalcedon. I am convinced it was her study of these historical events that led her to write the Apostles Creed inside her Bibles. That was pretty heretical for an old Baptist. Yet it showed her understanding that there was a necessary link between what we believe doctrinally and the historic events of the Christian church.

+++++

Streams of Living Water **by Richard Foster**

I was completely unaware of this book until I found it on Mom's bookshelf. Richard Foster is best known for his *Celebration of Disciplines*, which I discuss in Chapter 8. This book, written in 1998, is Foster's examination of the history of Christianity through six major traditions. He describes each of these as separate rivers which he believes are beginning to come together. The streams he describes are:

- The Contemplative Stream, the prayer-filled life.
- The Holiness Stream, the virtuous life.
- The Charismatic Stream, the Spirit empowered life.
- The Social Justice Stream, the compassionate life.
- The Evangelical Stream, the Word-centered life.
- The Incarnational Stream, the sacramental life.

In each of these areas Foster uses historical figures to show how the traditions developed and why they are important in the life of the church and the believer today. In the *Contemplative Stream* he refers to Antony, the ancient monk who spent 20 years in prayer and contemplation in the desert. Foster argues that this stream is important as a source of spiritual renewal for the church. It is an ancient tradition that has much to offer modern believers. It is a way of deepening our relationship with God and growing closer to him and is a way of engaging the spiritual realm and entering into the mystery of the divine.

Foster writes:

> *Every one of us is called to be a contemplative—not in the sense*
> *of a particular vocation we call "the contemplative life," but*
> *in the sense of a holy habit of contemplative love that leads*

us forth in partnership with God into creative and redeeming work. Thomas Merton writes, "I have not only repeated the affirmation that contemplation is real, but I have insisted on its simplicity, sobriety, humility, and its integration in 'normal Christian life.'" I invite you to the adventure of exploring in "normal Christian life" a loving attention to God and a growing union with God.

+++++

There's no question that the idea of the contemplative life appealed to mother. Her library was filled with books of prayers and short devotionals. Her poems reflected her thoughtfulness toward all things Christian. After the death of her husband in 1987, she began, I think, to take time daily for prayer and reflection. I don't mean that she became a hermit. She had lots of friends and enjoyed parties and dinners immensely. I just mean that, even at the end of her life, I could see her sitting quietly with a Bible or other book in her lap communing with her God.

+++++

With respect to the *Holiness Stream* Foster writes, "The Holiness Stream of Christian life and faith focuses upon the inward re-formation of the heart and the development of 'holy habits.'" Foster begins his discussion of this stream by tracing it back to Phoebe Palmer. Phoebe Palmer was a leader of the Holiness Movement in the 19th century. Her teachings, known as the Phoebe Palmer Theology, were influential in the development of the Holiness Movement and had a profound impact on the Wesleyan Church. She was born in New York City in 1807 to Methodist parents who were devoutly religious and encouraged her to pursue a religious life. She was an avid reader of religious literature and attended revival meetings, which had a profound impact on her spiritual life. In 1835, she had a powerful conversion experience and soon afterwards began to preach and teach. She was a passionate advocate for the Holiness Movement, which emphasized a life of holiness or sanctification, typically through prayer and Bible study.

Foster's reference to the holiness tradition is a reference to the Protestant Holiness Movement. This movement was a revival of the Wesleyan teaching that believers can experience a second work of grace, or entire sanctification, which is a state of moral perfection. It emphasizes a life of holiness or sanctification, typically through prayer and Bible study. Palmer wrote and published several books, including one of the most influential works on the Holiness Movement, "The Way of Holiness." Palmer was also a leader in the Methodist Women's Movement, advocating for greater opportunities for women to serve in the church. She was a major influence in the growth of the Holiness Movement throughout the world.

Foster attributes the Second Evangelical Awakening (1857 – 1865) to her ministry, which brought more than a million new converts into American churches. In the wake of her work in the British Isles, Foster says, from 1859 to 1863 more than 17,000 individuals professed their conversion to Christ.

Foster defines the Holiness Tradition in the following way:

> *Holiness means the ability to do what needs to be done when it needs to be done. It means being "response-able," able to respond appropriately to the demands of life. The word virtue comes into our New Testament from a long history in Greek philosophical tradition, and it means simply to function well. Virtue is good habits we can rely upon to make our life work. Conversely, vice is bad habits we can rely upon to make our life not work, to make it dysfunctional, as we say. So a holy life simply is a life that works.*

He then lists several key attributes:

- Holiness is not rules and regulations.
- Holiness is sustained attention to the heart.
- Holiness is not otherworldliness.
- Holiness is world-affirming.
- Holiness is not a consuming asceticism.
- Holiness is a bodily spirituality.
- Holiness is not works-righteousness.
- Holiness is a striving to enter in.
- Holiness is not perfectionism.
- Holiness is progress in purity and sanctity.
- Holiness is not absorption in God.
- Holiness is loving unity with God.

Foster concludes:

How wonderful to think that as we become partners with God, participating in this ongoing work of Christian perfection, our little light (which is not the source of light but only a reflection of the Light—and often a distorted and faint reflection at that) might lead others all the more fully to see Jesus, the Light of the world.

+++++

Foster writes of the *Charismatic Stream* that it "focuses upon the empowering charisms or gifts of the Spirit and the nurturing fruit of the Spirit. This Spirit-empowered way of living addresses the deep yearning for the immediacy of God's presence among his people." He begins his discussion of this traditions through examination of the New Testament references to the workings of the Holy Spirit. He also uses the example of Francis of Assisi who seemed to be especially empowered with the gifts of the Holy Spirit.

Foster also points to what is considered the new dawn of the working of the Holy Spirit in the contemporary world through an account of William Joseph Seymour and the Azusa Street Revival which began in 1906 in Los Angeles. It was at this revival that the full panoply of the gifts of the Holy Spirit came alive, including the practice of glossolalia, speaking in tongues. Foster writes:

> *A surge of interest brought huge crowds from virtually every race, nationality, and social class to Seymour's congregation. Meetings were held three times a day—morning, afternoon, and evening—often merging and flowing into one continuous worship experience from early morning to late night. The inside of the building overflowed with perhaps eight hundred persons, while four to five hundred more stood on the board sidewalk outside, squeezing together at the windows and doors in an attempt to see inside. These meetings continued on unabated for three years.*

Foster rightly reports that, as a result of the growth of this tradition since its Azusa Street beginnings, the Charismatic tradition has developed into a vibrant, diverse, and growing movement within the Christian faith throughout the world. It is best described as a revival movement that emphasizes a personal experience of the Holy Spirit. It is not limited to any one denomination or church. It is inclusive, drawing from a variety of Christian traditions and emphasizing the unity of all believers. It is marked by a powerful experience of the presence of God, often accompanied by the manifestation of spiritual gifts. Charismatic Christians seek to be obedient to the commands of Jesus and to be filled with the Holy Spirit. They focus on the power of prayer and the importance of living a life of holiness. Through the

Charismatic tradition, Christians can experience a deeper, more intimate relationship with God.

The spread of the Charismatic/Pentecostal stream over the past century has been nothing short of miraculous. Since the Azusa Street Revival in 1906 it has spread to nearly every corner of the world, with an estimated 500 million adherents worldwide. According to *Christianity Today* it has also diversified, with a variety of denominations, denominations within denominations, and independent churches. Pentecostalism has also grown in terms of its influence on other Christian denominations, leading to many churches adopting some of its distinctive practices, such as speaking in tongues and faith healing.

+++++

Foster perhaps glosses over the fact that Pentecostal practitioners were ridiculed and rejected by those in the mainline denominations. Baptists, in particular, seem to have been offended by charismatic practices. Mom, knowing that my wife Jane and I had been attending a Pentecostal church since the 1970s, told me a story from her youth about the Pentecostals in the small town of Breckenridge, Texas, where she grew up.

She said that, typically, on a summer Sunday evening in her town there was nothing at all to do. The movie theaters were closed. So she and her friends (the ones with cars) would drive to the parking lot of the little Pentecostal church in their town and they would sit outside the open windows (there was no air conditioning). Mom and her friends would laugh at the antics inside the little church, which she described to me as "whooping and hollering" and dancing around.

She seems, over the years, to have set aside her earlier disdain for this tradition, especially around me. But it is, I think, a fair description of the low regard toward Pentecostals historically held by most American Christians.

+++++

Foster's discussion of the *Social Justice Stream* begins with a history of John Woolman. Woolman was born in 1720 and was an American Quaker, abolitionist, and social reformer. He is best remembered for his work in advocating the abolition of slavery and his early stance against the slave trade (ChatGPT). He traveled throughout the American colonies and England, using his writings and personal visits to persuade slave owners to free their slaves. Woolman also advocated for fair treatment of Native Americans, women's rights, economic justice, and animal welfare. He was a leader in the Free Quaker movement, which sought to liberate Quakers from the restrictions of their own religious society. His book, *Some Considerations on the Keeping of Negroes*, is considered a major work in the history of American antislavery literature.

Foster also embeds this stream into the writings of the Old Testament prophet Amos who "declared in no uncertain terms that sacrifices, ceremonies, propitiations, and other externalities of religion were insufficient for a life with God." Foster maintains that this stream is to be characterized by the following:

1. A commitment to caring for the poor and vulnerable in society.
2. A focus on the common good and the well-being of all people.
3. An emphasis on the value of community and the importance of mutual aid and cooperation.
4. A belief that individuals have the right to participate in decision-making and have access to resources.
5. A recognition of the interconnectedness of the world and an

understanding that our actions have an impact on the lives of others.

6. A commitment to non-violent protest and advocacy for social change.
7. A responsibility to work toward a more just and equitable society.

Foster summarizes his key points as follows:

> *God calls us to a life of social justice whose circumference embraces 360 degrees: Personal, social, institutional. It is a life that receives all peoples: Enemies and friends, poor and rich, illiterate and educated, whomever and whomever. It is a life that engages in outward conflict with all social, economic, and civil injustices of society, judging down wickedness and building up the good, the true, and the beautiful.*

+++++

This "stream," as Foster describes it, is a bit more complicated in practice than he acknowledges. Almost all Christians understand that it is a responsibility of the church to care for those in need and to work diligently on behalf of those in our society being treated unjustly. Over the past century and a half, however, a divergence developed between those who saw the problem of the poor as essentially a moral one versus those who saw it as an organizational one. Some churches (the more evangelical ones) wanted to link their care for the needy with their efforts to evangelize while other churches (often in the mainline denominational tradition) wanted to organize institutional activities to help the poor without having to get directly involved themselves.

Mom would have none of any of that. Her church, Broadway Baptist, regularly provided meals for the homeless who inhabited the local area. She spoke to me many times of her absolute insistence that the feeding of the homeless at her church should never stop. She also believed it must always be a grace, a gift given without requiring any moral or spiritual response from the recipients. She understood, I think, that caring for the poor was not about the poor as much as it was about the spiritual impact on those who contributed to the work, who put together the meals, who handed them out, who cleaned up the mess. Social justice, for Mom, was for the givers. It was in the giving that they became more loving and caring and Christlike.

+++++

Foster addresses this issue of the disconnection that sometimes occurs between the *Social Justice Tradition* and the *Evangelical Tradition*. He writes: These two traditions—the *Social Justice Tradition* and the *Evangelical Tradition*—are at their best when they function together." Foster continues:

> *The Evangelical Tradition of Christian life and faith focuses upon the proclamation of the evangel, the good news of the gospel. We are enabled by the power of God to take the word of the gospel into our hearts in such a transforming way that others, seeing this, want it for themselves. This faith stream addresses the crying need for people to see the good news lived and hear the good news proclaimed.*

+++++

Foster uses two figures as metaphorical bookends for his discussion of the *Evangelical Stream*: St. Augustine and evangelist Billy Graham. He traces their coming to faith stories and their impact through the gospel tradition. Foster explains that the key features of the *Evangelical Stream* are:

1. The evangelical tradition is not simply a denomination, but a

global movement that crosses denominational and cultural boundaries.

2. The evangelical tradition is deeply rooted in the Bible, emphasizing the importance of personal faith and scripture study.

3. The evangelical tradition is embodied in six distinct "streams" of Christianity, including social holiness, pietism, evangelical activism, biblical literalism, prophetic faith, and pentecostalism.

4. Each stream has its own unique gifts, areas of emphasis, and historical context, but all share a common commitment to the gospel and to transforming the world.

5. Evangelicals have made significant contributions to culture, politics, and the academy, often challenging entrenched ideas and sparking debate.

6. The evangelical tradition must continue to embrace its rich heritage while also adapting to the changing context of the 21st century.

+++++

Mom's early religious life had clearly been rooted in the Evangelical Stream. That was what the King James faith and the Baptist churches of the mid twentieth century were all about. I don't think she ever rejected the truth the theology of that time embodied. But she clearly grew beyond it and maintained to the end that faith must actually do something constructive in the real world. If our hearts are changed by the good news, she would have said, that change compels us to reach out into our world and work to make it a better place.

+++++

The *Incarnational Stream*, according to Foster, is a way of making present and visible the realm of the invisible spirit. He writes, "This sacramental way of living addresses the crying need to experience God as truly manifest and notoriously active in daily life."

The incarnational stream of Christian spirituality can be reflected in worship by emphasizing the importance of connecting with God in a deep and meaningful way. This may involve recognizing the presence of God in the people and things in our lives and in the natural world around us. It may also involve engaging in worship practices that help us to remember the presence of God in our lives and to draw closer to Him. Examples of such practices may include singing hymns, participating in prayer, using Scripture in worship, and engaging in silence and reflection. All of these practices help to remind us of God's presence and to draw us closer to Him.

We tend to associate the incarnational stream with what might be called "high church" worship. That, as Foster points out, is not quite true. All churches, high and low, have an order to their worship. Most have prayers, singing, Bible reading, and preaching. This constitutes a liturgy. It is in this liturgy that God becomes present to us. Obviously, for some churches this is more deliberate than others, but it is present in all nevertheless.

Foster concludes:

> *All of us are called to sacramental living (incarnational). Redeemed by God through Christ, we are indwelt by the Holy Spirit and experience a growing transformation of character as our bodies come into a working harmony with our spirit. Hence our embodied self becomes a habitation of the Holy—a tabernacle—where we learn throughout our daily activities to function in cooperation with and in dependence upon God. Through time and experience we discover that everywhere we go is "holy ground" and everything we do is "sanctified action." The jagged line dividing the sacred and the secular becomes*

very dim indeed, for we know that nothing is outside the realm of God's purview and loving care.

+++++

Mom used to call her home church—Broadway Baptist Church—"high Baptist." She loved its Gothic-styled sanctuary, its beautiful organ and choir music deeply rooted in the classical tradition, and she loved its extensive use of liturgical elements in its worship drawn from a variety of source, but probably mostly from the Anglican *Book of Common Prayer.*

If I were to categorize her using Foster's paradigms, I would say that Mom was contemplative, evangelical, compassionate, and sacramental. I would put myself in different categories. I am evangelical, charismatic, and compassionate. Each of us has his own stream. It is important to remember, however, that each stream has its source in God and, we believe, will have its ending with God as well.

+++++

The Lost History of Christianity by Philip Jenkins

This book is not one that Mom would have purchased on her own, I think. It was one that I gave to her, and I was pleased to see that she deemed it worthy of her bookcase. The author, Philip Jenkins, is a distinguished professor of history at Baylor University and a fellow at the Institute for Studies of Religion. He has written widely on world religions and is the author of more than 30 books. He has also written for numerous publications, including *The New York Times*, The Wall Street Journal, and The Washington Post.

Jenkin's book is an important one because it dispels the myth of a Christianity that began in Palestine, spread throughout the Mediterranean, became centered in Rome, spread through Europe and into the New World, and finally was spread to Asia and Africa by means of various missionary movements. In fact, according to Jenkins, from the beginning Christianity was more dominant in the Near East and North Africa than it was in the West. The Books of Acts gives the impression that Christian missionary activity led west. In fact, many Christians in Palestine traveled east through Iraq and Iran where they built thriving Christian communities. Much of what is now the heartland of Islam was once thoroughly Christian.

In 780 c.e. Bishop Timothy became patriarch of the Church of the East, as it was known, which was then based at the Mesopotamian city of Seleucia. Timothy was the most significant Christian leader of his day, more important than the Pope in Rome or the Orthodox patriarch in Constantinople. According to Jenkins, a quarter of the world's Christians looked to Timothy as their spiritual leader. There were major learning centers in cities throughout the East, and Timothy himself presided over 85 bishoprics. In 1050, there were 373 bishoprics and the inhabitants of these areas were virtually all Christian. When Europe entered the dark ages, the intellectual life in the Christian East remained alive and well. Yet, a mere 400 years later, only 10 percent of the populations of the areas remained Christian

Everything had begun to change in 610 c.e. when the Prophet Muhammad received his first revelation from God and founded the Islam religion. Islam spread rapidly and violently, taking by force those areas that did not capitulate voluntarily. By 656 Islam had spread from the Arabian Peninsula to Baghdad. Cairo was taken in 969, and Constantinople itself, home of the Patriarch of the Orthodox Church, was taken in 1453.

For hundreds of years Muslims made accommodations for Christians throughout their areas of rule. Rulers appointed Christians as advisors and bureaucrats. But in the last few centuries this changed. Brutal campaigns led to the extermination of vast numbers of Christians so that today there are hardly any left of what was once the most Christianized area of the globe.

Jenkins' book on the history of Eastern Christianity gives lie to the idea that the Church is an ever-growing, ever-expanding entity. The Christian Church will die if we let it. I think Mom would have taken from this book the sense that we each need to fight for our churches, always working to make them better.

+++++

Mom loved Broadway and was a faithful member for 60 years. At Broadway she found a community of pilgrims seeking to find Jesus, a place of high worship, a place of prayer, and a church with a heart for the poor, the needy, the dispossessed.

Oddly, Mom complained to me a lot about her church. During her years at Broadway there were two great struggles that affected its life. (There may have been others. These are the ones she talked to me about.) First, there was a struggle over accepting women into the full ministerial life of the church. This began as a fight over whether women should be allowed to serve on the board of deacons and, over time, morphed into a fight over whether women should be allowed to work in the church in capacities other than children's ministry. By the time the dust had settled over the issue of the role of women in the life of the church, the gay issue popped up.

Over the course of the 60 years Mom was a member of Broadway, she saw waves of people leave in anger or frustration; she saw pastors fired and pastors chased off. In spite of the turmoil, Mom loved her church too much to leave it. And she spoke frequently of the need for churches to accept people where they are on their journey and to focus more on worshipping God than on fighting over issues that ultimately aren't so important.

I think Mom came to believe that being a member of a church was a lot like being a spouse in a bad marriage. When you get married, you are pretty naïve about all the deep-seated issues you're going to have to deal with in your relationship. There will be disagreements. But you compromise. You forgive. You value the relationship more than your personal desires on what, over the many decades of a marriage, turn out to be petty issues. Divorce was never an acceptable solution.

But Mom didn't just stick it out for better or worse; she worked really hard to make her church a better place for all who might enter its doors. She prayed for it. She gave money to it (that she could ill afford). She spent hours and hours of her time working on various church programs.

Mom used to visit other churches, particularly the larger, growing churches around town. She told me many times that the difference between successful churches and failing churches was the level of expectation each had of its members. Those who expected a lot grew. Those who expected nothing withered. She visited churches of all denominations (and a lot of nondenominational congregations). She visited synagogues. She visited high churches and non-liturgical churches. She wasn't bothered by doctrinal differences, but she was adamant that churches be kind and gracious and that they be involved in making the world a better place.

I found among Mom's papers a poem she wrote in 2014 entitled *The Church*:

> Not "my" church.

> But God's church.

Not this flawed gathering of wannabes

defined by men's dreams, limited by man's perspective.

This is God's church.

His Holy church—vast and timeless,

embracing every yesterday,

encompassing uncountable tomorrows.

Encircling all time and eternity.

It's God's Church.

It's magnificent.

And it's powerful!

The church that is the bedrock of faith.

The Benedictine Monks prayed:

"God, look not upon our sins but upon the faith of the church."

Marching through history we each bring our little crumb of faith,

far short of the powerful mustard seed.

But, ah! The strength of those crumbs *en masse*.

The power of all those crumbs collected through the ages. . .

enough to cover weakness, lack, flaws.

Power to give new life!

To bring forgiveness.

Move mountains.

To change men's lives.

The prayer of the monks becomes the prayer of the people:

"God, look not upon our sins but upon the faith of the church."

Chapter 7
The Inner Life: Some Old Classics

———

My journey through Mary's bookcase took me through her love of the Bible and allowed me to see how she used new translations and commentaries to grow beyond the simplistic "God said it and I believe it" mentality of her 1950s King James faith. And through a more complete knowledge of her reading about the church with its history and universality, I have come to a better understanding of her love of her church and her engagement with its liturgies, doctrines, and actions in its local community and in the world.

But Mom was not just about the Bible and church. There was a deeper element of her faith life. She didn't just read the Bible in a rote way; she prayed the Bible. She always took an extra moment to see if there was a deeper truth to be found in each passage.

And Mom prayed. When she moved in with my wife and me, I was surprised at how little time she spent watching television or reading for pleasure. When I entered her living area, I often found her quietly meditating (which she would gladly interrupt for a game of Scrabble). She seems to have kept an ever-expanding list of people and things to pray for. Her family. Her friends. Her church. My church. Strangers in need she heard about.

I was reminded of all this as I perused her bookcase, pulling out classic after classic, not sure where she found all these books. But they had one thing in common: They were directed at helping believers grow inwardly. These are not easy books. Their concepts require hard thinking. There are terms and phrases that need to be looked up. And they hold up a standard of living out the faith that seems overwhelmingly difficult to attain. Despite the fact that she had a very modest education, the presence of these books in her library suggests a powerful curiosity and intellect that I never appreciated when I was younger. Mom nevertheless seemed to have committed herself to the journey of spiritual self-enlightenment, not satisfied with the fare of standard Sunday sermons and Sunday School discussion groups. Each book she owned is worn, dogeared, and marked up. She obviously reread many of them.

In this chapter I have listed several of her books that might be considered older classics. Any Christian would be proud to have these in their library. The oldest are works by St. Augustine. The newest is by Dietrich Bonhoeffer. In the chapter which follows are some spirituality writings of a more recent vintage. All are treasures.

+++++

The Confessions of St. Augustine

Augustine was born in 354 c.e. in a Roman province in what is now Algeria (Wikipedia). His mother Monica, a powerful influence in his life, was a devout Christian. His father Patricius was a pagan who converted to Christianity on his deathbed. At the age of 11 Augustine was sent off to school where he became familiar with Latin literature along with pagan beliefs and practices. He seems to have been somewhat unruly and describes in his Confessions an episode when he and some friends stole some pears from a local garden. They didn't really want the pears, he wrote, but enjoyed the feeling they got from their thievery. He used this episode to elaborate on the innate attraction of sin.

At the age of 17 Augustine went to Carthage to continue his education in rhetoric. In spite of the warnings of his mother, he lived a hedonistic lifestyle for a time, associating with young men who boasted of their sexual exploits. While in Carthage he read Cicero's *Hortensius*, which seems to have encouraged in him a desire for greater wisdom and truth (philosophy). He began to teach, eventually moving from Carthage to Rome and then Milan.

While at Milan, Augustine's studies in Neoplatonism and his mother's faith encouraged him toward Christianity. It was his contact with an intellectual in Milan named Ambrose that helped him make his final commitment to the Christian faith in 386 at the age of 31. By 391 he was ordained a priest in Hippo in North Africa. He eventually became bishop. He wrote extensively and is considered one of Christianity's greatest theologians. He established the foundations of the Augustinian tradition of Christian thought, and his influence on the development of Western philosophy has been immense. He died in 430 in Hippo.

Confessions is an autobiographical work written by St. Augustine between 397 and 400. It is considered one of the most influential works of Western spirituality and theology. In it, Augustine reflects on his life, his struggles with sin and temptation, and his eventual conversion to Christianity. Augustine recounts his upbringing in a pagan household, his education in the Manichean religion, and his eventual conversion to Christianity.

Throughout his *Confessions* he speaks of sin in a very personal and reflective manner. He reflects on his own past sins of lust, pride, and greed, and his struggles with temptation. He expresses his deep remorse for his transgressions and his sorrow for the wrongs he has done. He also speaks of the power of sin, and how it can lead one astray from God and His will. He recognizes that it is only through repentance and faith that one can be saved and receive God's mercy and grace.

Augustine also speaks of the grace of God as a kindness and mercy that has been bestowed upon him, allowing him to be forgiven for his sins and receive the gift of salvation. He recognizes that it is only through God's grace that he can be saved and experience the joy and peace that comes with a life of faith. He expresses his deep gratitude to God for this gift, and for the mercy and love that He has shown him. Augustine's *Confessions* serve as a testament to the power of God's grace and the importance of repentance and faith.

+++++

Mom marked up her books as she pored over them. It's not easy to detect why one thing or another struck her fancy. In *Confessions* she underlined the following passage:

> *Lead us, O Lord, and work within us; arouse us, and call us back; enkindle us, and draw us to you; grow fragrant and sweet to us. Let us love you and let us run to you. Are there not many men who have turned back to you and drawn near to you? Are they not enlightened, as they receive your light? For if they receive it, they also receive from you power to become your sons. Yet if they are known to fewer people, so also those who know them rejoice less over them. For when many men rejoice together, there is a richer joy in each individual, since they enkindle themselves and they inflame one another.*

+++++

City of God by St. Augustine

In 312 c.e. the Roman Emperor Constantine converted to Christianity and made it the official religion of the empire. Emperor Theodosius I is credited with making Christianity the sole religion of the Roman Empire in 380 c.e. when he issued the Edict of Thessalonica, which declared Nicene Christianity as the only legally recognized faith in the Roman Empire. These events marked a major shift in the Roman Empire after centuries of Christian persecution, and it paved the way for the continued spread of Christianity throughout Europe.

Unfortunately, the Visigoths invaded Rome from the north and sacked the city in 410. (The emperors by this time were living in Byzantium in the East.) This event prompted many to question the very existence of the Christian God. Augustine wrote *City of God* between 413 and 426 to provide answers to these questions and to provide a philosophical and theological defense of Christianity in the face of continuing Roman paganism.

In *City of God* Augustine speaks of the existence of two cities: The earthly city and the City of God. By the "earthly city" Augustine refers to a society that is driven by earthly desires such as pride, greed, and violence. He argues that these desires prevent humans from achieving true happiness and fellowship with God. The earthly city is characterized by sin and corruption.

By the "City of God" Augustine refers to a society that is driven by divine love. He argues that this is the only true path to salvation, as it allows us to achieve true happiness and fellowship with God. The City of God is characterized by humility, charity, and peace, while the earthly city is characterized by pride, greed, and violence.

Augustine speaks of the ultimate goal of the City of God, which is eternal happiness and fellowship with God, and how this can only be achieved through faith and repentance. He also speaks of the power of grace, and how it allows us to be forgiven for our sins and receive the gift of salvation. *City of God* serves as a testament to Augustine's deep faith and commitment to God, and to the power of grace and mercy.

The key points Augustine makes in *City of God* are as follows:

1. There are two cities: The earthly city and the City of God.
2. The earthly city is driven by pride, greed, and violence, while the City of God is driven by humility, charity, and peace.
3. The ultimate goal of the City of God is eternal happiness and fellowship with God, and this can only be achieved through faith and repentance.
4. Grace is the power which allows us to be forgiven for our sins and receive the gift of salvation.
5. The City of God is the only true path to salvation.

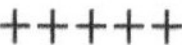

When Christianity was made the sole religion of the Roman Empire, it introduced a new way of practicing the faith that would, for better or worse, last for at least the next 1600 years. Roman officials began to use public monies to support the church and, simultaneously, to insert themselves into matters of church governance and doctrine. Some devoted Christians were horrified at this turn of events and fled into the desert where they could practice their faith without interference. The "desert fathers" ultimately morphed into the monastic movement which would be so important after the eventual fall of the Roman Empire. The majority of Christians breathed a sigh of relief at the end of the intermittent persecutions Christian had to endure, not fully understanding that political leaders in the centuries to come would clothe their naked exercise of power in the robe of Christianity as they went their merry way killing thousands upon thousands of those who were simply "other". Don't we weary of hearing about their atrocities of the Crusades, a clear legacy of the unholy alliance that developed between church and state.

Nevertheless, the pattern was set that there would be a symbiotic relationship between the governors and the church leadership. It was inconceivable that the crown would not be Christian or that the church would not support the state. We see the residue of this in those European countries where tax monies are used to support the church. Hitler had no problem coopting the National German church. The King of England is head of the Anglican Church, whether he wants to be or not.

When Mom entered adulthood in the mid-twentieth century, this Constantinian linkage was just beginning to break down in the U.S. The government, the media, and the education systems had for many years been supportive of Christian practices and values. The film industry paid a lot of attention to what the Catholic Church said was okay and what was not okay. Bishop Fulton Sheen had a prime-time television program that we used to watch. Billy Graham crusades were often broadcast. There were prayers and Bible readings every day in our schools. William Randolph Hearst, owner of a vast empire of newspapers put Billy Graham into the limelight with his famous telegram to his editors which read, "Puff Graham." Think of all the great colleges and universities that were founded by Christians. Think of all the parts of the health care system with the name "Saint" in their titles.

Over the course of Mom's adult life, it became increasingly clear that the structures of our civil society were no longer in the Christian camp. So once more St. Augustine's portrayal of the two cities has become relevant for the church and believers. The question to be answered is not whether we live in a Christian society, but how are we to live as Christians in Augustine's earthly city?

+++++

The Practice of the Presence of God **by Brother Lawrence**

The *Practice of the Presence of God* was written by a lay Carmelite in the 17th century. According to the preface to his book, we know that he was:

> *Born Nicholas Herman in French Lorraine, that he was lowly and unlearned in the teaching of the schools, that he served briefly as footman and soldier, and under the whips of God and conscience was driven to become a lay brother among the barefooted Carmelites at Paris in the year 1666 and was known forever after that as "Brother Lawrence."*

He was known for his simple, humble lifestyle and his dedication to the practice of living in the presence of God. He died in 1691, and his conversations and letters about the practice of the presence of God were edited and published after his death.

Brother Lawrence was a cook in the monastery. He was known for his ability to remain in a state of spiritual awareness and devotion while performing mundane tasks. He wrote that the practice of the presence of God should be applied to all aspects of life, including work. What are the key points in this book? *The Practice of the Presence* of God contains Brother Lawrence's advice on how to remain in the presence of God at all times. He encourages readers to practice this presence in all their activities, including work, prayer, and even mundane tasks. He also emphasizes the importance of humility, self-denial, and simplicity in order to stay focused on God and His will. He also encourages readers to trust in God's presence and guidance in all circumstances.

+++++

This is a very short book that can be read in less than an hour. Yet it is worth reading again and again. Its admonition to be constantly in communication with God reminds us of Paul's admonition to "Pray without ceasing."

Mom had marked several passages in this book that show her thinking about the spiritual matters offered by Brother Lawrence. I shall cite two of the passages taken from the letters included in the text:

He is always near you and with you; leave Him not alone. You would think it rude to leave a friend alone who came to visit you; why, then, must God be neglected? Do not, then, forget Him, but think on Him often, adore Him continually, live and die with Him; this is the glorious employment of a Christian. In a word, this is our profession; if we do not know it, we must learn it.

I must, in a little time, go to God. What comforts me in this life is that I now see Him by faith; and I see Him in such a manner as might make me say sometimes, 'I believe no more, but I see." I feel what faith teaches us, and in that assurance and that practice of faith I will live and die with Him.

+++++

The Cloud of Unknowing by Anonymous

Dark Night of the Soul by St. John of the Cross

The Cloud of Unknowing and *Dark Night of the Soul* are both spiritual works that explore the relationship between the individual and God. The *Cloud of Unknowing* is a 14th-century anonymous English work that focuses on the idea of *nepsis*, or a form of contemplative prayer meant to put the soul in a state of unknowing and surrender to divine grace. It encourages a seeker to focus on the love of God and to accept the unknown. *Dark Night of the Soul*, written by 16th-century Spanish mystic St. John of the Cross, is a poem that explores the spiritual journey, focusing on the idea of purgation, or the purifying of the soul in order to reach a state of union with God. It emphasizes detachment from the material world and the suffering of the soul as it progresses towards a greater spiritual understanding. Both works emphasize the need for faith and surrender to the unknown, but *The Cloud of Unknowing* focuses on nepsis and accepting the unknown, while *Dark Night of the Soul* emphasizes purgation and detachment from the material world.

Mom was passionate about prayer. She participated in retreats where prayer was the focus, she organized her own church's days of prayer, and she was diligent in her own private prayer life. She knew lots of people who were devoted to prayer, and they passed prayer requests around constantly. If you needed God's divine intervention in your life or the life of someone you loved, then a quick call to Mom would get a lot of people praying fervently and effectually. I frequently saw her with her prayer list, an odd assortment of needs that struck her fancy.

So it should be no surprise that she found herself in possession of these two medieval books on contemplative prayer. Unfortunately, neither is sufficiently coherent to make any sense to a modern reader. Mother certainly started *The Cloud of Unknowing*. She got through the Introduction which was written in 1922 by Evelyn Underhill. Ms. Underhill was an English writer and mystic. She was a leader in the modern revival of Christian mysticism and wrote extensively on the subject. Her introduction to the book was organized and lucid. Mom underlined passages extensively with plenty of sections underlined.

She managed to get through the first 24 pages of the text before she raised the white flag. My opinion is that, if you committed a felony and were sentenced to 10 years of solitary confinement, this might be the book to take with you. You could spend your entire prison sentence trying to read and grasp this book.

But Mom was not a quitter. She did what any intellectually curious OCD person would do. She got on the internet and found two articles explaining what the book was about. One of them was by Cynthia Blourgeault who used *The Cloud of Unknowing* as a resource for her own book *The Heart of Centering Prayer*. The other document did not include the name of the author but was an extensive outline of the key ideas in *The Cloud of Unknowing*. Mom printed these two documents out, folded them in half, and stuck them inside the front cover of the book. And *voila*!, an instant analysis of the book in case anyone ever asked about it.

I found an excellent review of The Cloud of Unknowing in one of my own books, *Longing for God: Seven Paths of Christian Devotion* by Richard J. Foster and Gayle D. Beebe. If I may quote a paragraph in the beginning section of their chapter on this work:

> *"The cloud of unknowing" is not a physical cloud but a darkness of understanding, a privation of knowledge. Our mind helps us understand that we lack knowledge and, also, that we will not penetrate the cloud with our mind but with our heart and the sharp darts of longing love. The cloud can be penetrated only when we quiet our mind and suspend our compulsion to prove everything rationally. The greatest temptation we face is to spend more time showing off our intellectual prowess than learning how to love God. The combined power of our intellect and pride become the greatest barrier to our life with God.*

There are six key points made in the book:

1. In order to truly experience God, one must empty the mind of all thoughts and be still.
2. The author recommends focusing on a "cloud of unknowing"—the idea that God is so far beyond human understanding that one must simply empty the mind and be still in order to experience Him.

3. Contemplative prayer is the practice of emptying the mind in order to experience God's presence.
4. God is beyond human understanding and can only be experienced by faith.
5. Prayer should be an act of love and adoration, not a tool of self-promotion.
6. The ultimate aim of prayer is to grow in a personal relationship with God.

The *Dark Night of the Soul* was written by the 16th-century Spanish mystic and poet St. John of the Cross. He became destitute at the age of three when his father died. He was taken in by the Jesuits who educated him. He met Teresa of Avilla who invited him to join the Carmelite order and bring it to men. He was a devoted disciple of Teresa of Avilla and worked tirelessly on her behalf. This support, and the opposition it soon bred, led to his death in 1591 at the age of 49.

He is one of the most influential figures in the history of Christian mysticism, and his works are widely read by those seeking spiritual guidance. He wrote extensively on the spiritual journey and is remembered as a devoted believer in the power of divine grace and the transformative potential of suffering. His intent in writing the *Dark Night of the Soul* was to describe the spiritual journey of one seeking union with God through a process of purification and transformation. He sought to provide guidance and support to those who were struggling with the difficult and often painful process of spiritual growth.

Mom managed to get a little further along in this book—to page 63 out of 184. I know this because she left her bookmark behind at that spot and her notes and underlining cease. There is a forward in the book by Thomas Moore. She certainly read that. I would refer readers to the

Foster and Beebe book for a cogent analysis of *Dark Night of the Soul.* Chat GPT lists 10 major points:

1. The Dark Night of the Soul is a spiritual crisis that can happen when one feels lost and disconnected from the Divine.
2. It is a time of intense spiritual purification where a person must confront their darkest fears, doubts, and pain.
3. It is a process of letting go of old patterns, beliefs, and attachments in order to discover a new and deeper sense of purpose and connection.
4. During this time, one may experience feelings of despair, hopelessness, and anguish as they search for a renewed sense of meaning and purpose.
5. It is essential to have faith during this time and to trust that the experience will bring transformation and renewal.
6. The person must open themselves up to the possibility of a new and transformed life in order to emerge from the dark night of the soul.
7. It is important to remember that the Dark Night of the Soul is a normal part of the spiritual journey and can be an opportunity for profound healing.
8. One should seek out spiritual guidance and support from friends, family, and mentors to help you through the process.
9. Remain open, receptive, and patient with yourself and the process.
10. Allow yourself to experience the full range of emotions and feelings without judgment.

+++++

At the end of the day, I think Mom left the ideas in these two works for others, not because she rejected them, but because her faith was too vibrant and other-oriented to spend much of her precious last few years in mystical contemplation. Mom cared about her community, her church, her family, and her friends. She prayed for them all daily. And she worked tirelessly to help everyone she could. She was, I think, at the end of it all a Brother Lawrence kind of Christian, communing constantly with God rather than a St. John of the Cross trying to let go of some dark despair. Mom had many difficulties in her life and, like all of us, suffered great losses. She simply didn't have time for despair and anguish. There were too many potatoes to peel.

+++++

The Christian's Secret of a Happy Life by Hannah Whithall Smith

To quote Foster and Beebe, "Hannah Whithall Smith, a Philadelphia Quaker, wrote *The Christian's Secret of a Happy Life*, which became a classic after it was published in 1870. Written from the perspective of Quaker simplicity and practicality, the book is a great encouragement to those who want to live a more joyful and fruitful life. Smith's secret to a happy life is to trust implicitly the promises of God."

The forward by the publisher of the book included the following paragraph about Ms. Smith:

> *She was a happy passenger in the chariot of God, always in the van and never a despondent straggler in the rear, calling out with an infectious enthusiasm, "Come up and ride with us!" She had nothing in common with the disillusioned author of Ecclesiastes, to whom "all, all is vanity," and all things filled with weariness. To her, every bush along the wayside was afire with God. There is a merry mercy, a rhapsodic joy in all she hears and sees and knows, for all, all is the handiwork of a God with a happy purpose for man, of a Creator who created all in beauty and in love. Life to her was no dismal journey between*

the peaks of birth and death; it was the scene of a continuing Triumphal Entry into the courts of God, with Everyman marching.

Unlike the previous classics on Mom's bookshelf, this one is cogent and coherent. She keeps scripture at the heart of her message (King James, of course). Yet she writes to ordinary people in ordinary circumstances. The publisher adds, "She writes here, not for the spiritual genius, not for the world-forsaking saint, but for those who are in the world and of it, for the great little ones who long for God as a struggle for bread."

Mom had her familiar markings in this book from front to back, so I know it was one she read and cared for. At the very beginning of the book is an extended passage that I would like to quote, because I think it touched Mom deeply. Ms. Smith wrote:

All of God's children, I am convinced, feel instinctively, in their moments of divine illumination, that a life of inward rest and outward victory is their inalienable birthright. Can you not remember, some of you, the shout of triumph your souls gave when you first became acquainted with the Lord Jesus, and had a glimpse of His mighty saving power? How sure you were of victory, then! How easy it seemed to be more than conquerors, through Him that loved you! Under the leadership of a Captain, who had never been foiled in battle, how could you dream of defeat? And yet, to many of you, how different has been your real experience! Your victories have been few and fleeting, your defeats many and disastrous. You have not lived as you feel children of God ought to live. You have had perhaps a clear understanding of doctrinal truths, but you have not come into possession of their life and power. You have rejoiced in your knowledge of the things revealed in the Scriptures but have not had a living realization of the things themselves, consciously felt in the soul. Christ is believed in, talked about, and served, but He is not known as the soul's actual and very life, abiding there forever, and revealing Himself there continually in His beauty. You have found Jesus as your Saviour from the penalty of sin, but you have not found Him as your Saviour from its power. You have carefully studied the Holy Scriptures and have gathered much precious truth therefrom, which you have trusted would feed and nourish your spiritual life, but in spite of it all, your souls are starving and dying within you, and you cry out in secret, again and again for that bread and water of life which you see provided in the Scriptures to all believers. In the very depths of your hearts, you know that your experience is not a Scriptural experience; that, as an old writer said, your religion is "bat a talk to whit the early Christians enjoyed, possessed, and lived in." And your hearts have sunk within you, as, day after day, and year after year, your early visions of triumph have seemed to grow more and more dim, and you have been forced to settle down to the conviction, that the best you can expect from your religion is a life of alternate failure and victory, one hour sinning, and the next repenting, and then beginning again, only to fail again, and again to repent.

I don't believe I've ever read anywhere a more nakedly truthful account of the experiences of most Christians as they struggle along their pilgrimage. A summary of Ms. Smith's solution to the dilemma may be summarized as follows:

1. True happiness is only found in submission to God.
2. The Christian life is a life of faith and trust in God.
3. The secret of happiness is found in daily surrendering and obedience to God's will.
4. God's blessing comes to those who believe in Him and trust

Him.

5. We must seek the Kingdom of God and His righteousness first in order to experience true joy and contentment.

6. We must focus on God's love and mercy, not on our own desires and expectations.

7. The Christian life is a life of service, not of selfishness.

8. We must be willing to sacrifice our own desires and plans in order to serve God.

9. We must seek to develop an inner life of prayer and meditation to draw near to God.

10. True peace can only be found in a life of surrender to God and His will.

Ms. Smith makes these points using many personal stories about her own life and people she has known. She includes many Bible references. Toward the end of the book Mom underlines the following paragraph:

> *The standard of practical holy living has been so low among Christians that the least degree of real devotedness of life and walk is looked upon with surprise and often even with disapprobation by a large portion of the Church. And, for the most part, the followers of the Lord Jesus Christ are satisfied with a life so conformed to the world, and so like it in almost every respect, that, to a casual observer, no difference is discernible.*

It's hard to believe this was written 150 years ago. It reminds me of the old quote, "The more things change, the more they stay the same." I would be remiss if I did not continue with Ms. Smith's following paragraph.

> *But we who have heard the call of our God to a life of entire consecration and perfect trust must do differently. We must*

come out from the world and be separate and must not be conformed to it in our characters or in our lives. We must set our affections on heavenly things, not on earthly ones, and must seek first the Kingdom of God and His righteousness; surrendering everything that would interfere with this. We must walk through the world as Christ walked. We must have the mind that was in Him. As pilgrims and strangers, we must abstain from fleshly lusts that war against the soul. As good soldiers of Jesus Christ, we must disentangle ourselves inwardly from the affairs of this life, that we may please Him who hath chosen us to be soldiers. We must abstain from all appearance of evil. We must be kind to one another, tender-hearted, forgiving one another, even as God, for Christ's sake, hath forgiven us. We must not resent injuries or unkindness, but must return good for evil, and turn the other cheek to the hand that smites us. We must take always the lowest place among our fellow men; and seek, not our own honor, but the honor of others. We must be gentle, and meek, and yielding; not standing up for our own rights, but for the rights of others. We must do everything, not for our own glory, but for the glory of God. And, to sum it all up, since He who hath called us is holy, so we must be holy in all manner of conversation; because it is written, Be ye holy, for I am holy."

Well said, Ms. Smith.

+++++

The Cost of Discipleship **by Dietrich Bonhoeffer**

Life together **by Dietrich Bonhoeffer**

We gain truth when we read the works of Dietrich Bonhoeffer, the German Lutheran pastor, theologian, anti-Nazi dissident, and founding member of the Confessing Church in Germany prior to the Second World War. But we realize the overwhelming power of his writings when we contemplate his death. Edwin Robertson quotes an account of Bonhoeffer's execution by an eyewitness—a prison camp physician—on the occasion of the execution:

> *On the morning of that day (April 9, 1945) between five and six o'clock the prisoners, among them Admiral Canaris, General Oster, General Thomas and Concillor of the German Supreme Court Sack, were taken from their cells, and the verdicts of the court martial read out to them. Through the half-open door in one room of the huts I saw Pastor Bonhoeffer, before taking off his prison garb, kneeling on the floor praying fervently to God. I was most deeply moved by the way this lovable man prayed, so devout and so certain that God heard his prayer. At the place of execution, he again said a short prayer and then climbed the place of execution, he again said a short prayer and then climbed the steps to the gallows, brave and composed. His death ensued after a few seconds. In the almost fifty years that I worked as a doctor, I have hardly ever seen a man die so entirely submissive to the will of God.*

He was born on February 4, 1906 in Breslau, Germany (now Wroclaw, Poland). His parents were Karl and Paula Bonhoeffer, who raised Dietrich and his siblings in a warm and loving home. Dietrich was academically gifted and excelled in school. He studied at the Universities of Tübingen, Berlin and Barcelona. He was ordained as a Lutheran minister in 1930 and soon after obtained his post-doctoral degree. In 1931, Dietrich became the pastor of two small churches in Berlin-Dahlem.

During this period, he wrote several influential works on theology, ethics, and the church's role in society. His first book, *The Cost of*

Discipleship, was published in 1937 and highlighted the importance of following Jesus' teachings and rejecting the materialism of modern society. Bonhoeffer was a vocal critic of the Nazi regime, publicly speaking out against the injustices of Adolf Hitler. During World War II he became an active member of the German resistance movement, working with other dissidents to plan Hitler's assassination. He was arrested in 1943 and executed in 1945, just weeks before the end of the war.

According to information in *Encyclopedia Britannica* (ChatGPT), Bonhoeffer, throughout his career, actively opposed Nazi ideology and spoke out against the persecution of Jews. Because the National German church had been coopted by the German authorities, he worked with the Confessing Church, a Protestant movement that opposed Nazi rule. He encouraged members to resist Nazi orders and to speak out against the regime's policies. He wrote several books and essays that exposed and criticized Nazi ideology and policies. He was involved in the formation of the German Resistance, a group of military officers and civilians who sought to overthrow the Nazi regime. He provided sanctuary and financial assistance to Jews who were fleeing from Nazi persecution. And he aided in the smuggling of Jews out of Germany and into neutral countries.

Fearful for his life, and rightly so, his friends persuaded him to flee Germany. It was arranged that he would teach at Union Theological Seminary in New York, which he did during 1939 and 1940. Interestingly, he found the large, mostly white, mainline churches in New York to be devoid of the gospel of faith, hope, and life that he so strongly believed in, so he spent his New York Sundays at The Abyssinian Baptist Church in Harlem.

In an astounding show of courage and an ever-present sense of love for his own German flock, he concluded that he simply could not be an effective pastor to the people of Germany after the war if he was unwilling to share their sufferings with them during the war. To the horror of those who loved and cared for him, he left the safety of New York and returned to Germany where his fate as a martyr was finally sealed.

The book for which he is best known is undoubtedly *The Cost of Discipleship* published in 1937. Mom's copy of this book is worn and marked and clearly loved. She paid $1.95 for it in 1974 and got her money's worth. I can barely keep its pages together as I peruse it to decipher Mom's notes. Its retirement is long overdue.

Bonhoeffer begins his book on discipleship with his famous contrast between cheap grace and costly grace. His opening line is a kill shot: "Cheap grace is the deadly enemy of our Church." He goes on to write:

> *Cheap grace means grace sold on the market like cheapjacks' wares. The sacraments, the forgiveness of sin, and the consolations of religion are thrown away at cut prices. Grace is represented as the Church's inexhaustive treasury, from which she showers blessings with generous hands, without asking questions or fixing limits. Grace without price, grace without cost!*

> *Cheap grace is the preaching of forgiveness without requiring repentance, baptism without church discipline, Communion without confession, absolution without personal confession. Cheap grace is grace without discipleship, grace without the cross, grace without Jesus Christ, living and incarnate.*

For Mom, as for many of us who grew up in the King James Protestant evangelical era, this picture of cheap grace is very close to what we were taught and believed. In fairness, many pastors and leaders would complain that it is a caricature of the doctrines of the Southern Baptist churches of the day. I'm sure there were Baptist seminary professors who were more sophisticated in their understanding of grace. But the *praxis* of the church in those mid-century days, was to sell a cheap grace at the door in the hopes that people would enter in and grow into disciples on their own. We wish we could say this is not also at the heart of some contemporary megachurches which slip so easily from true worship to mere entertainment.

Bonhoeffer goes on to contrast cheap grace with costly grace. He writes:

> *Costly grace is the treasure hidden in the field; for the sake of it a man will gladly go and sell all that he has. It is the pearl of great price to buy which the merchant will sell all his goods. It is the kingly rule of Christ, for whose sake a man will pluck out the eye which causes him to stumble, it is the call of Jesus Christ at which the disciple leaves his nets and follows him.*
>
> *Costly grace is the gospel which must be sought again and again, the gift which must be asked for, the door at which a man must knock.*
>
> *Such grace is costly because it calls us to follow, and it is grace because it calls us to follow Jesus Christ. It is costly because it cost a man his life, and it is grace because it gives a man the only true life. It is costly because it condemns sin, and grace because it justifies the sinner.*

What follows in his book is an extended commentary on Christian discipleship by Bonhoeffer using the beatitudes, sermon on the mount, and other passages from Matthew. They are worth reading again and again. Some of the ideas are difficult and deep and require thought. Overall, we can take from this work the following key ideas:

1. Discipleship requires a complete surrender of self-will, and obedience to the commands of Jesus.
2. Discipleship is costly and requires a life of self-denial and suffering.
3. The only way to follow Jesus is to take up our cross and follow him.
4. Discipleship involves living a life of humility and setting aside self-interests and ambitions.
5. We must not be afraid to stand up for truth and justice, even in the face of opposition and persecution.
6. Discipleship involves living a life of love and service, to our neighbors and to God.
7. Discipleship is a life-long journey and requires continual renewal and commitment.
8. We must always strive to live a life of holiness and purity, and to follow the example of Jesus.

+++++

In the United States in the 1960s vast social changes were beginning to appear in our politics and culture. The civil rights movements of the 1950s were resulting in major changes educationally, but progress was slow. Under President Johnson from 1964 through 1968 a variety of laws were passed to guarantee equal rights and equal access to public facilities. Johnson went even further with his Great Society programs designed to mitigate against the effects of the historic discrimination against black Americans for the entire century since the Civil War.

During those years my wife and I were attending a theologically liberal church in the mainline tradition and, more and more, we heard critiques about the "cheap grace" prevalent in many evangelical churches and the need to promote a newer "social gospel" to bring about equality of opportunity, fairness, and justice. Bonhoeffer's name was bandied about a lot.

There was certainly truth to the liberal complaint. Conservative evangelical churches were stuck in the rut of gaining members by the old process of getting professions of faith. They weren't really involved with the politics or social side of our nation's needs. In fairness, conservative Christians were doing a lot more than they were getting credit for. Who would deny the life-giving gospel work, for example, of the Salvation Army?

The heart of the problem for the "social gospel" churches was that they wanted to put in place programs to alleviate the ills of society disconnected from the life-transforming power offered through a knowledge of the saving grace of Jesus Christ. You can feed the poor all you want. But if you're not intimately involved in the lives of those you feed, you can feed them forever. You might feel good about that, but there's no "good news" in it. It's not "transformational," which it absolutely must be if it's truly an outworking of the Kingdom of God as Bonhoeffer would have understood it.

Many people inside the traditional King James churches immediately recognized the great truth Bonhoeffer was pointing out. Mom and others like her, committed Christians all, immediately saw the doctrinal flaws represented by cheap grace. And in Broadway Baptist Church and hundreds of others like it, there was a renewed emphasis on reaching out to those in need in their towns and communities with food, clothes, housing assistance, emergency financial aid, and other means of support. The most effective of these were about creating relationships through which the historic gospel message of the conservative churches could be communicated through their acts of charity. Sadly, one suspects a few couldn't help themselves from using good works to pressure poor souls into conversions.

+++++

Bonhoeffer formed the Confessing Church in April 1933 in response to the Nazi regime's efforts to control the German churches and impose Nazi ideology. The Confessing Church was an organized protest and a statement of resistance against the Nazi regime and became the focal point for religious opposition to the regime. Bonhoeffer sought to create a church with a strong commitment to its faith, independent from the state, and one that would not succumb to Nazi ideology. He hoped the Confessing Church would become a source of spiritual and moral strength in a time of turmoil and challenge.

In 1935 Bonhoeffer agreed to take charge of an "illegal" clandestine seminary for the training of young pastors to work in the Confessing Church. While there, he lived a common life in emergency-built houses with twenty-five vicars. He wrote about this time in his book *Life Together*. The key points are:

1. Community is essential for Christian life: Bonhoeffer emphasizes the importance of Christian community and its role in cultivating a deeper faith. He argues that living in community is essential for the Christian life and that individuals should strive to be in fellowship with others.

2. Christian community is a gift from God: Bonhoeffer argues that Christian community is a gift from God and that it should be treasured and cherished. He emphasizes the importance of fellowship, prayer, and worship in the life of a Christian community.

3. Life together in Christ: Bonhoeffer stresses the importance of living together in Christ and of being united with Him in all aspects of life. He argues that in order to live an authentic Christian life, individuals must make Jesus the center of their lives and strive to be obedient to His will.

4. The Cost of Discipleship: Bonhoeffer emphasizes the importance of taking up one's own cross and being willing to sacrifice for the sake of the gospel. He argues that true discipleship requires a willingness to lay down one's life in order to follow Christ.

5. The Nature of Love: Bonhoeffer emphasizes the importance of love in the life of the Christian community. He argues that love is the basis of Christian fellowship and that it should be expressed in the lives of all believers. He also stressed the importance of forgiveness and understanding in the life of a Christian community.

Mom had marked two passages in this book that I found illuminating. The first reads:

Christianity means community through Jesus Christ and in Jesus Christ. No Christian community is more or less than this. Whether it be a brief, single encounter or the daily fellowship of years, Christian community is only this. We belong to one another only through and in Jesus Christ.

What does this mean? It means, first, that a Christian needs others because of Jesus Christ. It means, second, that a Christian comes to others only through Jesus Christ. It means, third, that in Jesus Christ we have been chose from eternity, accepted in time, and united for eternity.

The second passage, oddly, is about the role of silence in our common worship:

There is an indifferent, or even negative, attitude toward silence which sees in it a disparagement of God's revelation in the Word. This is the view which misinterprets silence as a ceremonial gesture, as a mystical desire to get beyond the Word. This is to miss the essential relationship of silence to the Word. Silence is the simple stillness of the individual under the Word of God. We are silent before hearing the Word because our thoughts are already directed to the Word, as a child is quiet when he enters his father's room. We are silent after hearing the Word because the Word is still speaking and dwelling within us. We are silent at the beginning of the day because God should have the first Word and we are silent before going to sleep because the last Word also belongs to God. We keep silence solely for the sake of the Word, and therefore not in order to show disregard for the Word but rather to honor and receive it.

+++++

These classic books seemed to open a door for Mom to what would become the most important element of her spiritual life—how she experienced the life of Christ on the inside so that it showed on the outside. I think she began to see that understanding the Bible, King James or otherwise, and knowing how the church and its doctrines inform our worship and our faith practice were all well and good. But at the end of the day, we need to be transformed from the inside out. And we need to do that by cooperating with the Holy Spirit. We don't just lay back and let God do all the work. Once saved, always saved, who cares about the rest? No. We study, we pray, we sit in silence, we tend to the wounds of others, whether we feel like it or not. We give generously when and where we can—of time as well as treasure. We forgive. We confess. And somewhere along the line God in his infinite wisdom begins to change us ever so slowly into the image of his dear son and our Savior, the Lord Jesus Christ.

Mom did not believe she had reached the pinnacle of the spiritual journey as we sat and visited in our North Carolina home on those last few days of her 98 years. She admitted to a lot of failings. But she was, I think, about as close to the spiritual mountaintop as you could get.

Chapter 8
The Inner Life: Some New Friends

In the last chapter I focused on Mary's library of older classics as they related to the development of the inner life of Christians as they travel on their pilgrimage of faith. In Mom's collection of current books are more than I can competently cover in a single chapter. So I have selected four works that I think were most influential to her as she thought about growing her life from the inside out.

I would like to point out that that Mom acquired these books when she was in her 70s and 80s. There was no sense in her that there was a retirement age for the true apprentice of Jesus. One toils until the day is done. I would also note, somewhat facetiously, her oft-repeated claim that authors really only have one book in them, and you can get the gist of that book just by reading the first and last chapter. The rest is just publishers trying to get some extra money.

I am going to review four of the books from her collection that I think she considered important. I have selected them because they were so extensively marked. They include *Celebration of Discipline* by Richard Foster, *Renovation of the Heart* by Dallas Willard, *Care of the Soul* by Thomas More, and *The Rule of Benedict* by Joan Chittister. I would be remiss if I did not mention several other authors for whom she had multiple books in her collection. Readers may wish to see for themselves why she kept them with her to the very end. They include the writings of M. Craig Barnes, Henri J.M. Nouwen, Elizabeth O'Conner. There is certainly treasure in these works as well.

+++++

***Celebration of Discipline: The Path to Spiritual Growth* by Richard J. Foster**

***Renovation of the Heart* by Dallas Willard**

I am taking these two books as a unit for two reasons. First, they supplement each other in important ways. And secondly, Richard J. Foster and Dallas Willard were close colleagues.

Richard J. Foster is a best-selling author, speaker, and founder of Renovaré, a movement that offers resources for cultivating a life of spiritual transformation. Foster has written multiple books on Christianity, but the best known is *Celebration of Discipline*, which has sold more than 2 million copies and has been translated into over twenty languages. Foster holds a degree in philosophy from Yale University and a doctorate in history of religion from Fuller Theological Seminary. He has served as a pastor and professor of spiritual formation at several institutions, including George Fox University and Regent College.

I first read *Celebration of Discipline* in the 1980s and immediately hated it. I thought it had two flaws. It smacked of sugar-coated self-righteousness and it seemed elitist. Despite Foster's best efforts to say his approach to spiritual development did not involve following a bunch of rules, as you read through the book what you see are a bunch of rules. Set aside a specific time to pray. Get into a good position. Pick a verse. Meditate on it. There's fasting and study and confession and prayer. It all seemed like a bunch of work and, dare I say, slightly Pharisaical. The last thing an old Baptist wants to be is a Pharisee.

My other complaint was that it seemed designed for pastors and teachers and people without a lot to do all day. (I know that's a myth.) Good for them. I had a two-hour commute to Washington every workday. As a small business owner I put in 10 or more hours of work a day. With four daughters we had music lessons and sports stuff. I was a DIY king, especially dealing with the yard and plumbing. After we did church, I couldn't see how I was ever going to sit in silence and meditate for more than five minutes a month. Give me Brother Lawrence any day, chopping up those potatoes with God in his heart and by his side.

But then I began to read a little bit by Dallas Williard. Dallas Willard (1935-2013) was an American philosopher and Christian teacher who wrote extensively on the nature of Christian discipleship. He was a professor at the University of Southern California, where he taught in the School of Philosophy, Religion, and Humanities.

Willard's key ideas focused on spiritual formation and discipleship. He argued that spiritual formation and discipleship are essential parts of a Christian's life, and that they should be the focus of Christian ministry. He also believed that the goal of Christian discipleship is to enable us to know God, to live in harmony with his will, and to experience the fullness of life he offers. He argued that spiritual transformation is only possible through a life of prayer, study of scripture, and service to others. He advocated for a holistic approach to discipleship, involving the integration of all aspects of life, including our physical, mental, and spiritual health. He emphasized the importance of community and of being part of a church family. Finally, he argued that spiritual formation is not a one-time event, but an ongoing process of transformation.

I read two books by Willard not on Mom's bookshelf. I know that she read them as well because I let her borrow my copies, and we discussed them on occasion. One is the *Divine Conspiracy* and the other is *The Spirit of the Disciplines*. Both are great books, but in the second he speaks out against what he called "sin management."

Willard's concept of "sin management" is based on his understanding that sin is more than simply breaking a moral rule or committing an act of wrongdoing. It is a matter of spiritual formation and transformation, as it is rooted in a person's internal motivations and desires. He argues that sin management must involve more than simply identifying and avoiding wrong actions; rather, it must involve a process of spiritual formation and transformation that leads to a deeper, more authentic relationship with God. This process involves a commitment to disciplines that help the individual to address the underlying motivations and desires that lead to sin.

In *Renovation of the Heart* Willard speaks of the need to, first, change the heart and only then try to change our habits and practices of life so we are strengthened on the inside in His power rather than trying to change on the outside by our own power.

As I suspect many readers did as well, I was reading Foster as a kind of spirituality for dummies. Do A, B, and C and you get instant spirituality. I should have understood that, as was Willard, Foster was trying to get me to focus on my heart, because that is where the real change needed to take place. I also, over time, have come to see that I may have made some poor life choices that led me to complain about the "elitism" I saw in his writing. I believe that, not in an evil or conscious way, I chose my manner of living freely and was running like the hamster in the wheel trying to keep up with no time left over for God, my own spiritual well-being, or my family. At the age of 80, I do not wish I had spent more time at work.

Foster lists 12 historic disciplines for consideration. They are:

1. Meditation
2. Prayer
3. Fasting
4. Study

5. Simplicity
6. Solitude
7. Submission
8. Service
9. Confession
10. Worship
11. Guidance
12. Celebration

Readers, if they have not already done so, may wish to study these on their own. For now, however, I want to note some of the ideas Mom felt were worth underlining as she journeyed through Foster's book.

+++++

Mom's Notes on Meditation

Perhaps somewhere in the subterranean chambers of your life you have heard the call to deeper, fuller living. You have become weary of frothy experiences and shallow teaching. Every now and then you have caught glimpses, hints of something more than you have known. Inwardly you long to launch out into the deep.

Those who have heard the distant call deep within and who desire to explore the world of the Spiritual Disciplines are immediately faced with two difficulties. The first is philosophic. The materialist base of our age has become so pervasive that it has given people grave doubts about the ability to reach beyond the physical world.

The second difficult is a practical one. We simply do not know how to go about exploring the inward life. This has not always been true. In the first century and earlier, it was not necessary to give instruction on how to "do" the disciplines of the spiritual life. The Bible called people to such disciplines as fasting, prayer, worship, and celebration but gave almost no instruction about how to do them. The reason for this is easy to see. Those disciplines were so frequently practiced and such a part of the general culture that the "how to" was common knowledge. Fasting, for example, was so common that no one had to ask what to eat before a fast, or how to break a fast, or how to avoid dizziness while fasting—everyone already knew.

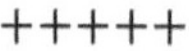

God has given us the disciplines of the spiritual life as a means of receiving his grace. The disciplines allow us to place ourselves before God so that he can transform us.

+++++

A farmer is helpless to grow grain; all he can do is provide the right conditions for the growing of grain.

The disciplines are God's way to getting us into the ground; they put us where he can work within us and transform us. By themselves, the spiritual disciplines can do nothing; they can only get us to the place where something can be done. They are God's means of grace.

+++++

When we genuinely believe that inner transformation is God's work and not ours, we can put to rest our passion to set others straight.

Leo Tolstoy observes, "Everybody thinks of changing humanity and nobody thinks of changing himself.

+++++

The Bible uses two difference Hebrew words to convey the idea of meditation, and together they are used some 58 times. These words have various meanings: listening to God's word, reflecting on God's works, rehearing God's deeds, ruminating on God's law, and more. In each case there is stress upon changed behavior as a result of our encounter with the living God. Repentance and obedience are essential features in any biblical understanding of meditation.

+++++

Christian meditation, very simply, is the ability to hear God's voice and obey his word. (Mom wrote: hear and do).

+++++

What happens in meditation is that we create the emotional and spiritual space which allows Christ to construct an inner sanctuary in the heart.

+++++

Her Notes on Prayer

To pray is to change. Prayer is the central avenue God uses to transform us. If we are unwilling to change, we will abandon prayer as a noticeable characteristic of our lives. The closer we come to the heartbeat of God the more we see our need and the more we desire to be conformed to Christ.

Usually, the courage actually to go and pray for a person is a sign of sufficient faith. Frequently our lack is not of faith but of compassion.

Her Notes on Study

We must understand, however, that a vast difference exists between the study of scripture and the devotional reading of scripture. In the study of scripture, a high priority is placed upon interpretation: What it means. In the devotional reading of scripture, a high priority is placed upon application: What it means for me.

When we study a book of the Bible we are seeking to be controlled by the intent of the author. We are determined to hear what he is saying, not what we want him to say. We want life-transforming truth, not just good feelings. We are willing to pay the price of barren day after barren day until the meaning is clear. This process revolutionizes our lives.

Her Notes on Simplicity

Mom had few material possessions. My father's illness had cost them much of their savings, so she lived simply. Her notes on possessions were meaningful:

1. Receive what we have as a gift from God.
2. To know that it is God's business, and not ours, to care for what we have.
3. To have our goods available to others.

From Foster she noted that we should:

1. Buy things for their usefulness rather than their status.

2. Reject anything that is producing an addiction in you.
3. Develop a habit of giving things away.
4. Refuse to be propagandized by the custodians of modern gadgetry.
5. Learn to enjoy things without owning them.
6. Develop a deeper appreciation for the creation.

+++++

At the end, I believe Mom's spirituality was deeply embedded in the thought and ideas of Richard Foster in his *Celebration of Disciplines*. It seems to represent the best that we can find in our complex, high-stress world: A call to set aside time and space for mending the wounds of our soul, in preparation for new forays into the world as it actually exists. Spiritual formation, ultimately, is organic. It grows slowly but surely from the inside out.

+++++

The Care of the Soul by Thomas Moore

THOMAS MOORE WAS A best-selling author, psychotherapist, and lecturer who wrote the book *Care of the Soul: A Guide for Cultivating Depth and Sacredness in Everyday Life*. It was first published in 1992 and has since become a classic of spiritual and psychological self-care. Moore lived as a monk in a Catholic religious order for 12 years and has degrees in theology, musicology, and philosophy.

According to Moore the soul is a precious and delicate thing that should be treated with reverence and respect. It must be tended to with care and attention and be given the time and space it needs to thrive. He believed we should pay attention to our dreams, fantasies, and imaginative life as sources of insight and meaning. According to Moore we are all unique and our individual paths should be honored and celebrated. We should use our creative abilities to express our deepest feelings and desires. We should strive to live a meaningful and fulfilling life by engaging in activities that bring us joy and satisfaction. We should embrace our imperfections and vulnerabilities and learn to accept and love ourselves for who we are. We should strive to cultivate a healthy balance between body and soul by cultivating meaningful relationships, engaging in meaningful activities, and taking time for self-care. We should strive to live in harmony with the natural world and take care of our environment.

Moore's book, while a source of many important ideas, seems a bit too pop psychology for Mom. She clearly read it and marked it up, but I don't think it held a central place in her thinking in quite the same way that Richard Foster did.

+++++

The Rule of Benedict by Joan Chittister

The Rule of Benedict by Joan Chittister is a modern interpretation of the sixth-century Benedictine rule, which is an ancient monastic code of conduct. Joan Chittister is an American Benedictine nun, author, and speaker. She was born in 1936 in Erie, Pennsylvania, and joined the Benedictine Sisters at the age of 18. She holds a master's degree in theology and a doctorate in speech communication from Penn State University. She has published over 50 books and is a frequent public speaker on topics such as spirituality, justice, and human rights.

Chittister's interpretation of the Rule of Benedict focuses on how the principles of hospitality, humility, obedience, and stability can be applied to everyday life. She argues that these principles can help individuals lead a balanced, meaningful, and reflective life. Chittister emphasizes the importance of silence, contemplation, and respect for one another, and she offers guidance on how to cultivate a spiritual practice. Ultimately, she encourages readers to use the Rule of Benedict as a source of spiritual nourishment and a tool for personal growth.

Mom loved all things monastic, so it's not hard to see why she gravitated to this book. Based on the notes in the margins, I believe Mom may have used it as a teaching guide for a class she led for her church or other Christian group.

The main areas that Mom seemed to have ben interested in are drawn from the section on humility. I'm uncertain why this would be. Chittister wrote:

> *If the twentieth century has lost anything that needs to be rediscovered, if the Western world has denied anything that needs to be owned, if individuals have rejected anything that needs to be professed again, if the preservation of the globe in the twenty-first century requires anything of the past at all, it may well be the commitment of the Rule of Benedict to humility.*

The author is referring, of course, to the Rule of Saint Benedict, a book of precepts written by Benedict of Nursia in the sixth century for monks living in community under the authority of an abbot. It is one of the most influential religious rules in Western Christendom and has been a guiding force in the formation of religious communities for centuries. The Rule of Saint Benedict outlines the norms of monastic life, which includes principles of humility, obedience, prayer, and stability.

Mom highlighted from this book 12 steps of humility:

1. The first step of humility, then, is that we keep "the reverence of God always before our eyes" and never forget it.

2. The second step of humility is that we love not our own will nor take pleasure in the satisfaction of our desires.

3. The third step of humility is that we submit to the prioress or abbot in all obedience for the love of God, imitating Jesus Christ, of whom the apostle says: "Christ became obedient even to death."

4. The fourth step of humility is that in this obedience under difficult, unfavorable, or even unjust conditions, our hearts quietly embrace suffering and endure it without weakening or seeking escape.

5. The fifth step of humility is that we do not conceal from the abbot or prioress any sinful thoughts entering our hearts, or any wrongs committed in secret, but rather confess them humbly.

6. The sixth step of humility is that we are content with the lowest and most menial treatment and regard ourselves as a poor and worthless worker in whatever task we are given.

7. The seventh step of humility is that we not only admit with our tongues but are also convinced in our hearts that we are inferior to all and of less value, humbling ourselves.

8. The eighth step of humility is that we do only what is endorsed by the common rule of the monastery and the example set by the prioress or abbot.

9. The ninth step of humility is that we control our tongues and remain silent, not speaking unless asked a question.

10. The tenth step of humility is that we are not given to ready laughter.

11. The eleventh step of humility is that we speak gently and without laughter, seriously and with becoming modesty, fairly and reasonably, but without raising our voices.

12. The twelfth step of humility is that we always manifest humility in our bearing no less than in our hearts.

I can see Mom's struggles in these steps. Mom was, despite her lack of formal education, a proud woman. She challenged authority, particularly if she thought they were trying to sell her a bill of goods. She had a sharp tongue, but it was accompanied by a raucous laughter. She was impish and fun loving. Yet, I suspect, she saw the value in many of these rules. How well she integrated them into her life is another question.

+++++

In these last two chapters I have been looking at the books that may have influenced her in terms of her own personal spiritual growth. I don't believe that the mysticism in *Dark Night of the Soul* or *The Cloud of Unknowing* resonated with her. I think she was much more comfortable with Brother Lawrence, with Hannah Whitehall Smith, and especially with Richard Foster. These were ideas one can live with in the twenty-first century. I don't think she practiced all the disciplines delineated in these books, but she daily sought God's presence, she made her own quiet time, and she prayed.

I also think central place in her theology should be given to Bonhoeffer's *Cost of Discipleship*. If there is any concept that stands over and against the literalistic fundamentalism of Mom's early life, it would have been that of "costly grace." She knew intellectually and intuitively that, while God's grace was freely given, it also placed a call on our lives that requires an answer. If we want God's freely given grace in our lives, we are compelled to offer the price it demands in terms of personal sacrifice. Not as payment, but as gift.

Chapter 9
Ethics

Mary was fiercely ethical in her personal life. There was no room for gray. There was no middle ground when it came to honesty. She was particularly careful to make sure every debt was paid to the penny (financial and otherwise). Unfortunately, Christianity itself is a little more vague when it comes to rules of behavior.

One of the things that Christianity does very badly is rules. We don't like them. The Christian writings, sadly to say, carry an undercurrent of antisemitism built around the "yeast of the Pharisees," that is, hypocrisy. There are historical reasons for this antipathy between early Christians and first century Jews, and it is a tragedy that it has played itself out with such vehement antisemitism ever since.

From the beginning the early Christians saw that a major failing of the prevailing Jewish culture was its commitment to a legalism that missed completely the underlying heart of the faith, especially with respect to such things as mercy, grace, forgiveness, justice. The call of Jesus was a call to the heart to love and to forgive. Christians, particularly in Paul's writings, railed against legalism (circumcision) and what has come to be called "works righteousness."

In this theological system, every attempt to put into place some rule seems to stand against freedom and grace. In the mid-twentieth century in the Baptist church there were two big rules. No drinking and no dancing. I remember asking a Bible teacher about drinking wine, since it seems clearly mentioned in the Bible. His answer was that they were using grape juice, not wine. Even at the age of nine I knew that was probably not true.

My point is that Christians over the years have lost the ability to think and act ethically in the same way that our Jewish friends are able to do.

Mom had in her possession the book *Jewish Wisdom* by Rabbi Joseph Telushkin. This is a wonderful book, and I am delighted that she kept it in her collection. Telushkin is an American rabbi and bestselling author who is best known for his books on Jewish ethics and values. While Christians have spent the last two millenia rejecting legalism, the Jews have spent the last 3,000 years thinking carefully about right and wrong behavior in every possible human circumstance. It's clear from this book that these are not "legalistic" arguments being made. They are being made from the heart, with the greatest good and dignity of all taking primacy.

The central Hebrew text is the Torah, the first five books of the Hebrew scriptures. It is here that the earliest Jewish commandments make their appearance. The remaining portion of the Hebrew scriptures include the writings and the prophets. Taken together, these three sections of scripture are called the Tanakh.

In addition, there are additional sources of wisdom referred to as the Talmud. The Talmud includes lengthy disputes concerning Jewish law as well as stories and anecdotes. There are two versions of the Talmud, a Babylonian Talmud and a Palestinian Talmud. The Babylonian is the more authoritative. In addition, there is a document referred to as the Mishna, which classifies Jewish law into sixty-three discrete, short books.

Taking all these documents together, Telushkin describes hundreds of ethical and moral dilemmas and shows what the ancient wisdom has to say about it. The book is organized into eight larger sections:

1. Between People: How to be a good person in a complicated world.
2. Personal Issues: Judaism and the quest for meaning.
3. Between People and God: What God wants from us.
4. Between People and the World: Jewish values confront modern values.
5. Modern Jewish Experience: Major themes.
6. The Holocaust
7. Zionism and Israel.
8. On Being a Jew: Modern reflections.

There is too much information here for me to do justice to any one topic, but, because Mom was always concerned about the need to care for the homeless and others in need, I would like to quote some passages from Telushkin's section on "helping the helpless."

Telushkin begins this section by quoting German-Jewish philosopher Hermann Cohen (1842 – 1918) who claimed that the biblical commandments protecting the stranger represented the beginning of true religion:

> *The stranger was to be protected, although he was not a member of one's family, clan, religion, community, or people; simply because he was a human being. In the stranger, therefore, man discovered the idea of humanity.*

Telushkin repeats a section from a Yom Kippur sermon given by Rabbi Robert Kirschner on AIDS in 1985 in San Francisco:

> *Where [our sages asked] shall we look for the Messiah? Shall the Messiah come to us on clouds of glory, robed in majesty, and crowned with light? The Babylonian Talmud reports that*

Rabbi Joshua ben Levi put this question to no less an authority than the prophet Elijah himself.

Where, Rabbi Joshua asked, shall I find the Messiah?

At the gate of the city, Elijah replied.

How shall I recognize him?

He is among the lepers.

Among the lepers? Cried Rabbi Joshua. What is he doing there?

He changes their bandages, Elijah answered. He changes them one by one.

This may not seem like much for a Messiah to be doing. But, apparently, in the eyes of God, it is a mighty thing indeed.

And another story:

A similar story tells of Rabbi Salanter, eating a meal at another's house, and surprising everyone present by using a minimal amount of water in the ceremonial washing of the hands before the blessing over the bread. The others, who had lavishly poured water over their outstretched hands, asked him to explain his unusual behavior.

I noticed that a maid brings the water up to the house in buckets drawn from the well. Those buckets are very heavy, and I don't want to perform my mitzvah on her shoulders.

+++++

Mom was never antisemitic, and I know she enjoyed these stories from Rabbi Telushkin. One of her quirky habits had to do with her ethnicity. Mom had a dark complexion and tanned easily. Occasionally, some nitwit would ask her if she were Mexican. "Oh, no," she would reply. "I'm Jewish." But if the nitwit in question happened to ask if she were Jewish, she would invariably answer, "Oh, no. I'm Mexican." Mom's family was thoroughly English.

There are two approaches to ethics that find their way into the Christian ethos. The first is referred to as deontological ethics. The second is consequentialism. Deontological ethics are those rules of behavior that are deemed to be right or wrong without regard for their consequences. Idolatry is forbidden as an integral component of the Christian faith. Part of being Christian is to reject the worship of other gods. The ten commandments are typically taken to be rules that are to be followed without regard for consequences.

On the other hand, there is a school of thought which says that an act is to be judged based on its consequences. Is anyone hurt by this? If not, so what?

The conservative Christianity of the 1950s and 1960s said, for example, that killing in war was okay, capital punishment was okay, ordinary murder was not okay, and (eventually) abortion was not okay. This gets complicated. Is killing in self-defense okay (probably)? Is killing to protect property okay (maybe)?

My conversations with Mom over the last 18 months of her life led me to believe she made her ethical decisions out of an inner core of values deeply influenced by the heart of the scriptures. In Matthew we hear Jesus saying, *Thou shalt love the Lord thy God with all thy heart, and with all thy soul, and with all thy strength, and with all thy mind; and thy neighbor as thyself.*

There were five things I would say about Mom's ethics:

1. When she saw what she called "misbehavior" in others, she did not judge or condemn. I think a lifetime of struggling with relationship issues and disappointment gave Mom a sense that we need to show a bit of grace to those who lose their way.

2. She did not think God was petty. Many of our failings might violate one rule or another in the Bible, but in the grand scheme of things, they are small and silly sins, not worth a lifetime of *mea culpas*. I think her attitude was, get over it and move on. Do better next time.

3. She did not care for those who seemed committed to justifying their obnoxious behavior. Admit you were wrong. Don't do it again. Get on with life.

4. She believed that God cares more about the condition of the heart that gives rise to our foolish behavior than he does about the bad behavior itself. Grace. Mercy. Dignity. Humanity. All the things we see in Rabbi Telushkin's book Mom seemed to hold dear.

5. Repentance and forgiveness ought always to be at the center of the Christian life of faith. At the end, Mom knew her time was short, and she was quick to use it to forgive all those who had wronged her. And I know that, in her heart of hearts, she sought forgiveness from those she had wronged.

6. Mom understood that "rules" were not the coin of the realm in God's Kingdom. Ultimately, it is the attitude of the heart that allows us to find our way forward.

+++++

When I was young we attended a small Baptist church out in the country west of Fort Worth. There was a young man who was a member of the church who worked as a dance instructor at a local Arthur Murray dance studio. The senior members of the church decided that this was a sinful lifestyle and that he needed to find a different line of work. When he did not, they voted him out of the church. I understand today that he was almost certainly gay. However, that was not mentioned at the time.

I don't recall any discussions of this with Mom at the time, but I know that she would have been horrified by this toward the end of her life. She had moved beyond the hypocritical fundamentalism of her early years and cared deeply about the people in her social circle. She worked to get the justice. She prayed for them. She mentored them. And, above all, she loved them.

+++++

Can You Drink the Cup by Henri Nouwen

Mom had several books in her possession by Henri J.M. Nouwen. Nouwen, who died in 1996, was a Dutch Catholic priest, professor, writer, theologian, and spiritual director whose life and work profoundly impacted the contemporary Christian spiritual landscape. He was born in the Netherlands in 1932 and grew up in a Catholic family. After studying philosophy and theology at Catholic University in Nijmegen, he was ordained as a priest in 1957. He then left his homeland to study psychology at the University of Louvain in Belgium, where he received his PhD in 1965. Nouwen went on to teach at the University of Notre Dame and Harvard Divinity School, and later served as the pastor at the University of L'Arche Daybreak in Richmond Hill, Ontario.

L'Arche is an international network of communities where people with and without intellectual disabilities share life together. Nouwen's ministry there focused on deepening relationships, expressing love, and creating a sense of belonging. He worked at L'Arche Daybreak in Richmond Hill, Ontario, for the last fourteen years of his life.

The book by Nouwen that Mom seemed most drawn to was *Can You Drink the Cup* published in 1996. Mom had a strong affection for the disabled. She started a program for the disabled at her home church. I suspect her interest was triggered by the birth of a severely disabled grandchild.

Can You Drink This Cup is a collection of Henri Nouwen's reflections on the spiritual lifein which he explores the tension that exists between the desire to be faithful to God and the challenge of facing the difficulties and suffering of life. He encourages readers to embrace their spiritual journey, even when it is difficult, and to remain open to God's presence in all circumstances. The book offers inspiring words of wisdom and comfort to those seeking to deepen their connection with God.

Mom had read it carefully, marking the passages that spoke to her. I would like to quote several of them at length.

> *One thing I learned from it all: drinking wine is more than just drinking. You have to know what you are drinking, and you have to be able to talk about it. Similarly, just living life is not enough. We must know what we are living. A life that is not reflected upon isn't worth living. It belongs to the essence of being human that we contemplate our life, think about it, discuss it, evaluate it, and form opinions about it.*

> *The greatest joy as well as the greatest pain of living come not only from what we live but even more from how we think and feel about what we are living. Poverty and wealth, success and failure, beauty and ugliness aren't just the facts of life. They are realities that are lived very differently by different people,*

depending on the way they are placed in the larger scheme of things.

Reflection is essential for growth, development, and change. It is the unique power of the human person.

Our cup is often so full of pain that joy seems completely unreachable. When we are crushed like grapes, we cannot think of the wine we will become. The sorrow overwhelms us, makes us throw ourselves on the ground, face down, and sweat drops of blood. Then we need to be reminded that our cup of sorrow is also our cup of joy and that one day we will be able to taste the joy as fully as we now taste the sorrow.

We need to remind each other that the cup of sorrow is also the cup of joy, that precisely what causes us sadness can become the fertile ground for gladness. Indeed, we need to be angels for each other, to give each other strength and consolation. Because only when we fully realize that the cup of life is not only a cup of sorrow but also a cup of joy will we be able to drink it.

Nothing is sweet or easy about community. Community is a fellowship of people who do not hide their joys and sorrows but make them visible to each other in a gesture of hope. In community we say: "Life is full of gains and losses, joys and sorrows, ups and down—but we do not have to live it alone. We want to drink our cup together and thus celebrate the truth that the wounds of our individual lives, which seem intolerable when lived alone, become sources of healing when we live them as part of a fellowship of mutual care."

We truly need each other to claim all of our lives and to live them to the fullest. We need each other to move beyond our guilt and shame and to become grateful, not just for our successes and accomplishments but also for our failures and shortcomings. We need to be able to let our tears flow freely, tears of sorrow as well as tears of joy, tears that are as rain on dry ground. As we thus live our lives for each other, we can truly say: "To life," because all we have lived now becomes the fertile soil for the future.

And finally:

We have to drink our cup slowly, tasting every mouthful—all the way to the bottom! Living a complete life is drinking our cup until it is empty, trusting that God will fill it with everlasting life.

+++++

Leap Over a Wall by Eugene H. Peterson

This book has a subtitle that I think turned it into a book Mom kept on her bookshelf instead of putting it aside as just another attempt by an established author to sell a few more books. The full title of the book is *Leap Over a Wall: Earthy Spirituality for Everyday Christians*. In the same way that Mom related to the ancient book by Brother Lawrence, she related to a book grounded in the reality of the world as it truly is and as it is experienced by ordinary believers.

The book is based on the life of King David, one of the Bible's most important figures. Peterson draws on the example of David to illustrate how faith and an open heart can lead to spiritual renewal and joy. He discusses how David faced his fears and faced the unknown with courage, and how trusting in God's love and guidance can lead us on a path of spiritual growth. Peterson also uses David's life to illustrate how to be a faithful Christian, and to show the importance of trusting in God's plan. Peterson tells his story through David's interactions with the people who were important in his life: Samuel, Saul, Jonathan, Abigail, Nathan, Mephibosheth, Bathsheba, Absalom, Abishag, and others.

Peterson points out that David's story, from beginning to end, is completely without miracles. In fact, Christians are often drawn to David's story because nowhere else in the Bible do we find such an unvarnished account of the life of a person of faith. David's life is replete with love and hate, anger, violence, lust, murder, and various assorted sins of the flesh. It is also full of regret, repentance, and forgiveness. Peterson uses the word "earthy" to describe David, and he certainly was.

By "earthy spirituality," Peterson is referring to a spiritual practice that is grounded in the physical world and the everyday life of a Christian. This practice involves engaging with the world around us, taking time to reflect on our faith and to explore the depths of our spiritual life. Peterson encourages readers to take a leap of faith and to be open to the beauty and mystery of the world around us. He encourages us to be mindful of our spiritual journey and to seek out opportunities for spiritual growth and renewal.

Peterson asks the question early in the book, "Why David?" He gives this answer in a passage Mom had marked:

> *There are several strands that make up the answer, but prominent among them is David's earthiness. He is so emphatically human: David fighting, praying, loving, sinning. David conditioned by the morals and assumptions of a brutal Iron Age culture. David with his eight wives. David angry; David devious; David generous; David dancing. There's nothing, absolutely nothing, that God can't and doesn't use to work his salvation and holiness into our lives. If we're going*

to get the most out of Jesus' story, we'll want first to soak our imaginations in the David story.

Afterward

I well remember standing at the foot of Mom's bed in the hospital on January 30, 2022, as her breathing faltered and her heart slowed. I knew it was the end. As is often the case in such circumstances, she seemed so small in the bed for such an oversized figure in life. She had been unconscious for two days and passed quietly on that Sunday morning.

I had been given a great privilege over the prior 18 months. Each morning Mom and I sat together while she drank her coffee, and we chatted about all the odds and ends of life. Sometimes we talked about old family things. Sometimes we talked about faith things. I wish I had been paying better attention to her words, but we never do really. It's only later that we have that thought. After going through all her notes and books and after thinking about our conversations, it seems fair to ask what life lessons Mom really wanted to leave as her legacy.

+++++

Mom was a believer in and follower of Jesus of Nazareth. She didn't just acknowledge his existence and move on. She saw him as her personal Messiah and followed him as an apprentice follows after the master craftsman. She had been to Jerusalem and had walked the paths he walked. She studied scriptures diligently to understand the key events of his life and the theological and historical context of his story. She listened to his voice in the gospel accounts. She visited the historical sites of his passion, his crucifixion, his resurrection.

And she did not flinch at the claims that Jesus was raised from the dead. I know this because she had written in her own hand the words of the Apostle's Creed inside her Bible. This was her faith foundation and it had been since she was baptized as a child at Cliff Temple Baptist Church in Dallas. She never wavered in that belief.

She had no interest in those who claimed to be Christian simply because their parents had raised them in the church or because they had good programs for the kids or because it just seemed like a good place to network. Neither did she have any interest in those who claimed to be Christian but had no interest in joining other believers on their pilgrimage of faith. Mom wanted to hang out with the true believers, the committed, those whose decision to follow Jesus was deep and profound.

She, of course, tolerated those who just seemed to be hanging on in the faith. Show up on Christmas and Easter. Give a little money now and then. Get your kids in the youth group and hope for the best. But what she really hoped for and worked for and prayed for was that lightening would strike and, by the grace of God, even these religious dilettantes would finally come to see what true Christianity was all about.

+++++

Mom was not dogmatic in her beliefs. In fact, she could change what she thought about faith things from day to day. We often discussed various Bible passages, and she was able to hold together two different ideas: Did this event really happen as it is described in the Bible? And whether it actually happened or not, what is the great truth God wants us to learn from this story. It wasn't faith-changing for her if she thought a particular Bible story might not be literally true, because she always looked past the words of the text to the underlying truth. Having said that, in subsequent discussions her faith would often reassert itself and she would claim absolutely that a particular Bible story was historically true.

I will say this. People who study the Bible for a couple of hours a day for 90 years or so are not people who don't believe the words of it contain profound truths worthy of the search. Mom and I used to watch church services together on television each Sunday morning (because of COVID). Rarely did she get through a sermon without wanting to stop and look up some scripture or another that she thought was being misused or mischaracterized. Sometimes she was right and sometimes she was wrong. But it was the Bible itself that was her yardstick for truth. In general, I think she took scripture as essentially true and built her faith life around that.

I think she would say this to skeptics: Take the Bible as a whole. Find its overarching message. Interpret individual stories in the context of this greater truth. And, for her, she held on to the Apostles' Creed as a kind of boundary beyond which speculation ought not to go.

Mom also found it useful to read what other people thought about a particular passage. She may or may not have agreed with them (she rarely agreed with anybody), but she was always open to new understandings about a particular passage. So she read commentaries and books on the Bible, underlining and making notes as she went. She truly had an insatiable appetite for all things Biblical.

+++++

Mom believed deeply in the church. She understood that there are lots of different kinds of churches and she never considered any particular church or denomination to be "right". There certainly are good churches and not so good churches. They are big or little, rich and poor, high church and low church, loud and quiet. Good music and otherwise. Just as there are good pastors and pastors who struggle to get a coherent thought out of their mouths. Mom believed every person who professed to be Christian belonged in a church that they could claim as their own. For better or worse. Because, ultimately, it is the relationships that believers build in the church with each other that get them through all the difficult stages of their lives.

In Mom's world, it was not possible to be truly Christian apart from a Christian community. She saw church attendance as the modern equivalent of the old Jewish sacrificial system. Families would go up to the Temple to offer a sacrifice. It was a requirement of being Jewish. This sacrifice could not have cost nothing. Otherwise, it was not a sacrifice. You had to give up something for it to be efficacious. Going to church each week to offer your worship is the modern equivalent. You give up an hour of your time on Sunday morning to sit with other believers, sing hymns, listen to Bible reading, hear a sermon. On a good day, you might confess your sins. On a bad day, you might just be numb. You might be bored and your mind might wander. But you are there with God, and you are there with other pilgrims seeking to find God afresh. That is the call of church. That is why Mom drove herself to church every Sunday morning in her little Mazda well into her nineties. It was her worship and her sacrifice.

I can say from experience that, when illness and death finally overtake us, it is nice to have a church to call. A family of fellow believers who can walk us through the grief of death just as a good church walks us through the pain and suffering of life. There's nothing worse than a funeral when the officiant admits that he (or she) never really met the person but by all accounts they seemed like they were nice. (They probably weren't all that nice.) No. You want to be surrounded by people who knew you and loved you.

+++++

Mom believed that, sooner or later, if you regularly attend a particular church you will need to assume some responsibilities for making it a better place. That, for her, meant supporting it with money and supporting it with your time. Mom did both, and she did it her entire adult life.

For the last few years of Mom's life I was a cosigner on her checking account. Her only income was Social Security and the interest on a small amount of money tied up in certificates of deposit. I noticed that twice each year she made a contribution of $500 to Broadway Baptist Church. I'm not sure how she came up with that amount, but it was faithfully given and was not money she could easily afford. Nevertheless, she gave it gladly. One thinks of the widow's mite.

Mom also had a long history of devoting her time and energy to various church projects. She led a Bible study. She organized prayer events. She led fund-raising efforts. She once took a group down to New Orleans after Katrina to hold Vacation Bible School for local churches. She organized a class for the disabled. Mom got a lot from her church through the years, but she put a lot into it as well.

+++++

Mom believed that forgiveness, grace, and mercy were foundational elements for the Christian life. She lived the Sermon on the Mount, although with some fits and starts. Toward the end of her life she shared some of her regrets and she mentioned to me some of people she forgave for the wrongs they had done to her.

Oddly, there was one person she claimed she would never forgive. I think she was joking about it, but, with Mom, you couldn't always be sure. When she was in her early nineties, she decided to buy a new car. Ever independent, she didn't bother to consult with her children. She studied her options online and decided on a particular model of Mazda. She always thought of herself as a hard bargainer, so she went to the dealership with her price in mind. The salesperson found just the car she wanted. As they negotiated over the price, unbeknownst to

Mom, each time Mom offered a price that was lower than the salesman was asking, he responded by taking away some feature on the car. After she paid and picked up the car, she realized the car had been stripped of many of the features she wanted. She told me that she would never forgive that salesman and, if he ever showed up at her church, she would walk out. I knew two things to be true. That car salesman was never going to show up at Broadway Baptist Church and, if he did, Mom would have been gracious to him.

Life can be difficult. Few of us manage to get through it without finding ourselves in conflict with someone. Sometimes it's our fault and sometimes it's not. But there is a pain that we carry for each broken and bruised relationship we leave behind us. The Bible is clear that the anger and bitterness that follow from such broken relationships damage even the essence of our relationship with God Himself. So we are told to forgive. We're not told how. That is part of what it means to be a pilgrim.

+++++

Mom was never satisfied with where she was spiritually. There was always some new Bible passage to study and digest. There was always some new book to read. And there were a lot of old books to read again and again where you might find a key to help you understand a little better what God is trying to say to you. It's that spirit of openness that kept her mind sharp and her spirit strong to the very end.

+++++

I think Mom would have said this to each member of her family: You come from a Christian home. Your parents were Christian, as were their parents before them. That is your legacy. No matter where you find yourself in life today, no matter what failures you have experienced, no matter what pain you have suffered, there is before you a door that can only be opened by you. The glorified, resurrected Jesus stands at that door waiting for you to open it and join him. He has a journey he wants to take with you. It will be greater that any journey you can imagine, full of twists and turns, joy and pain. But the end will be worth it, because that is where you will find Mom and all the other saints of the church universal and historic waiting to welcome you to the home you have always longed for but could never find. That is where you can finally put your burdens down and rest.

Selected Bibliography

Daniell. D. (Translator) (1989). *Tyndale's New Testament.* New Haven: Yale University Press.

Anonymous. (2017). *The Cloud of Unknowing.* Middletown, DE.

Augustine, S. (1958). *City of God.* City, N.Y.: Image Books.

Augustine, S. (1960). *The Confesions of St. Augustine.* Garden City, New York: Image Books.

Bonhoeffer, D. (1954). *Life Together.* New York: Harper&Row Publishers.

Bonhoeffer, D. (1974). *The Cost of Discipleship.* New York: MacMillan Publishing Co., Inc.

Chittister, J. (2009). *The Rule of Benedict: Insights for the Ages.* New York: Crossroads Publishing Company.

Cross, S. J. (2003). *Dark Night of the Soul.* New York: The Berkley Publishing Company.

Eusebius. (1999). *The Church History.* Grand Rapids, Michigan: Kregel Publications.

Foster, R. J. (1988). *Celebration of Discipline: The Path to Spiritual Growth.* New York: HarperCollins Publishers.

Foster, R. J. (1998). *Streams of Living Water: Clelbrating the Great Traditions of Christian Faith.* San Francisco: HarperSanFrancisco.

Gonzalez, J. L. (2010). *The Story of Christianity (Volumes I and II).* New York: HarperCollins.

Hebrew-English Tanakh. (1999). Philadelphia: The Jewish Publication Society.

Jenkins, P. (2008). *The Lost History of Christianity.* New York: HarperCollins.

Josephus, F. (1998). *Josephus.* Nashville: Thomas Nelson.

Moore, T. (1994). *Care of the Soul: A Guide for Cultivating Depth and Sacredness in Everyday Life.* New York: HarperCollins.

Nouwen, H. J. (1996). *Can You Drink the Cup?* Notre Dame, Indiana: Ave Maria Press.

Ogilvie, L. J. (1983). *The Communicator's Commentary: Acts.* Word, Inc.

Peterson, E. H. (1997). *Leap Over a Wall.* New York: HarperCollins.

Peterson, E. H. (2002). *The Message: The Bible in Contemporary Language.* Colorado Springs, Colorado: NavPres.

Raymond E. Brown, J. A. (1968). *The Jerome Biblical Commentary.* Englewood Cliffs, N.J.: Prentice-Hall, Inc.

Smith, H. W. (1870). *The Christian's Secret of a Happy Life*. Westwood, N.J.: Fleming H. Revell Company.

Telushkin, J. (1994). *Jewish Wisdom*. New York: William Morrow and company, Inc.

The Amplified Bible. (1965). Grand Rapids, Michigan: Zondervan Bible Publishers.

The Holy Bible: New Internatonal Version. (1986). Grand Rapids, Michigan: Zondervan Bible Publishers.

The Holy Bible: Revised Standard Version. (1971). Iowa Falls, Iowa: World Bible Publishers.

The Jerusalem Bible. (1971). Garden City, Ne York: Double & Company, Inc.

The Living Bible. (1971). Wheaton, Illinois: Tyndale House Publishers.

The Master Bible. (1941). Chicago: J. Wesley Dickson & Co.

The Septuagint. (2016). Peabody, Massachusetts: Hendrickson Publishers Marketing.

Underhill, E. (1994). *Abba*. Harrisburg, Pa.: Morehouse Publishing.

Willard, D. (2002). *Renovation of the Heart: Putting on the Character of Christ*. Colorado Springs: NavPress.

Yonge, C. (2016). *The Works of Philo*. Hendrickson Publishers Marketing, Inc.

Young, R. (1977). *Analytical Concordance to the Bible.* Grand Rapids, Michigan: Wm. B. Eerdmans Publishing Company.